I0822061

EUCHARISTIC ADORATION

Scriptural Reflections and Prayers

Jesus, I adore you.

EUCHARISTIC ADORATION

Scriptural Reflections and Prayers

Most Rev. Arthur J. Serratelli
S.T.D., S.S.L., D.D.

•

CATHOLIC BOOK PUBLISHING CORP.
New Jersey

NIHIL OBSTAT: Rev. T. Kevin Corcoran, S.T.D., MA
Censor Librorum

IMPRIMATUR: ✠ David M. O'Connell, C.M., J.C.D., D.D.
Bishop of Trenton

September 8, 2021

The Nihil Obstat and Imprimatur are official declarations that a book or pamphlet is free of doctrinal or moral error. No implication is contained therein that those who have granted the Nihil Obstat and Imprimatur agree with the contents, opinions or statements expressed.

(T-947)

ISBN 978-1-953152-60-2

Totowa, NJ 07512

Printed in Korea

catholicbookpublishing.com

Contents

Introduction

At seven o'clock in the evening on August 18, 1996, Fr. Alejandro Pezet was saying Mass in the commercial center of Buenos Aires. After he finished distributing Holy Communion, a woman came up to tell him that she had found a discarded host on a candle holder at the back of the church. Fr. Alejandro took the defiled Host and placed it in a container of water in the tabernacle.

On Monday, August 26, upon opening the tabernacle, he saw to his amazement that the Host had turned into a bloody substance. He informed Cardinal Jorge Bergoglio (the future Pope Francis) that the Host had become a fragment of bloodied flesh and had grown significantly in size. It was decided to keep it in the tabernacle. After three years passed and the Host had suffered no visible decomposition, Cardinal Bergoglio decided to have it scientifically analyzed.

In 1999, in the presence of then Cardinal Bergoglio, Dr. Ricardo Castanon, an atheist at the time, sent the fragment to New York for analysis. Not to prejudice the issue, no information about the origin of the fragment was given to the team of scientists. One scientist, Dr. Frederic Zugibe, a cardiologist and forensic pathologist, determined that the substance was real flesh, containing human DNA. He further concluded that it was a piece of a heart that had been tortured. Amazingly, the samples were even pulsating while they were being studied. The blood was discovered to have AB blood type. This perfectly matched the scientific studies done on the Eucharistic miracle of Lanciano.

Over the centuries, there have been miracles of the Eucharist. Lanciano in the 8th century. Bolsena and Santarém in the 13th century. Siena in the 18th century. And even in our lifetime: Finca Betania in Cúa in 1991; Tixtla, Mexico in 2006; and, Saint Anthony of Sokółka, Poland in 2008. In each and every case, the Church has submitted these miracles to the careful scrutiny of science. And the results have been the same. Real flesh. Real blood.

Yet, even before the first Eucharistic miracle, the Church was always teaching that the Eucharist is truly the Body and Blood of Jesus under the appearance of bread and wine. In his letter to the Romans (106 A.D.), St. Ignatius of Antioch says, “I desire the bread of God, the heavenly bread, the bread of life, which is the flesh of Jesus Christ, the Son of God, who became afterwards of the seed of David and Abraham; and I desire the drink of God, namely His blood, which is incorruptible love and eternal life." For the first 1,000 years the Church, both in the East and the West, tenaciously held to this belief that the Eucharist is the Body and Blood of Jesus.

However, in the 11th century, Berengar, a priest of Tours and a leading scholar at the Cathedral school of Chartres, taught that Christ was only spiritually present in the Eucharist and that the elements of bread and wine remained. For thirty years, theologians argued and debated, trying to clarify the Church's faith. At four different councils, Berengar's teaching was condemned: at Brionne, at Chartres, in Rome, and at Vercelli.

Hildebert de Lavardin, Archbishop of Tours, who had been a pupil of Berengar, answered the arguments of his famous teacher. He introduced the term "transubstantiation" to describe the change of bread and wine into the Body and Blood of Christ at the consecration of Mass. Almost immediately thereafter, the Fourth Lateran Council used this term for the first time in a statement of the magisterium. On November 11, 1215, the Council affirmed that "Christ's Body and Blood are truly contained in the sacrament of the altar under the forms of bread and wine, the bread and wine having been transubstantiated, by God's power, into his Body and Blood."

Except for a very few theologians, the doctrine of the Real Presence of Jesus went undisputed for more than 500 years. Then came Luther and the Protestant reformers. Luther taught that the bread remains bread and the wine remains wine, but that Jesus becomes present in those elements at the moment of the reception of Holy Communion. Thus, he taught something of a real presence but not as the Church teaches.

Other reformers went further than Luther and completely denied the Real Presence. Calvinists speak of receiving Christ in a spiritual and heavenly manner. They teach that, even after the consecration, the bread and wine remain the bread and wine. The Methodists, Baptists, Disciples of Christ, and Mennonites consider the Lord's Supper a simple memorial service. Anglicans are divided among themselves. Some hold to transubstantiation; others do not. And, the Quakers and the Salvation Army have no Eucharist at all.

Nonetheless, from the moment the apostles gathered with Jesus in the Upper Room to the most recently celebrated Mass, the Church has steadfastly held to the literal meaning of Jesus' words. After the priest repeats Jesus' words "This is my Body...This is my Blood," only the appearance of bread and wine remain. The reality, the substance, is changed. It is *the Body of Christ*. It is *the Blood of Christ*.

Even before the gospels were written, Paul wrote about the Eucharist. He was very clear in how he described the elements. In 1 Cor 11:27, Paul says, "Anyone who eats the bread and drinks the cup of the Lord in an unworthy manner is guilty of an offense against the body and blood of the Lord." Obviously, Paul believed in the Real Presence.

In response to the Protestant reformers who were denying the Real Presence, the Council of Trent clearly and unequivocally enunciated the Church's faith. The Council taught that, in the Eucharist, "the body and blood, together with the soul and divinity, of our Lord Jesus Christ and, therefore, the whole Christ is truly, really, and substantially contained." Recognizing that it is the Lord himself, Jesus, our Savior and Judge whom we receive, before receiving Holy Communion, wc rcpcat the words of the centurion in the gospel, "Lord, I am not worthy that you should come under my roof, but only say the word and my soul shall be healed." We come humbly before the Lord who loves us so much to give us Himself.

In the Eucharist, the Son of God comes to be one with us. The celebration of the Eucharist is the supreme act of worship of the Church. And, that act of worship is prolonged in the adoration of Jesus in the Blessed Sacrament. By it, we continue our union with Jesus and we also prepare ourselves for receiving Holy Communion. In fact, "No one eats that flesh without first adoring it" (St. Augustine, *Expositions on the Psalms*, 98:9).

When we adore the Eucharist outside of Mass, we remain in intimate contact with Jesus, the wellspring of all grace. The Eucharist is Jesus the child who was conceived of the Virgin Mary and born in Bethlehem. It is Jesus the Teacher who spent three years preaching the kingdom of God. It is Jesus the Healer who brought wholeness to the bodies and hearts of those oppressed. The Eucharist is Jesus who shed His blood on the Cross, rose from the dead and is now seated at the right hand of the Father. Thus, both in the reception and the adoration of the Eucharist, Jesus touches us and transforms us with all the mysteries of His life, death, and resurrection.

> *It is not just while the Sacrifice is being offered and the Sacrament is being confected, but also after the Sacrifice has been offered and the Sacrament confected—while the Eucharist is reserved in churches or oratories—that Christ is truly Emmanuel, which means "God with us." For He is in the midst of us day and night; He dwells in us with the*

fullness of grace and of truth (68). He raises the level of morals, fosters virtue, comforts the sorrowful, strengthens the weak and stirs up all those who draw near to Him to imitate Him, so that they may learn from His example to be meek and humble of heart, and to seek not their own interests but those of God.

Pope St. Paul VI, *Mysterium Fidei*, 67

When we come before the Blessed Sacrament with our prayers of petition, reparation, thanksgiving and adoration, we place ourselves next to the heart of Jesus just as John the Beloved Disciple did at the Last Supper. "Of all devotions, that of adoring Jesus in the Blessed Sacrament is the greatest after the sacraments, the one dearest to God and the one most helpful to us" (St. Alphonse Liguori). It allows Jesus to draw us into the mystery of His own divine life, making us His Body, the Church in the world.

The following scriptural reflections are offered as a way to deepen our understanding and appreciation of the great sacrament of the Eucharist. They examine and explain the meaning and purpose of the Eucharist in God's plan for our salvation. When used in meditation and prayer before Jesus truly present in the Eucharist, they provide an opportunity for us to become truly alive to God and to others. Adoration of the Eucharist is our heart gazing on the Lord in faith and trust. It is the look of love that draws us into deeper union with Jesus. As St. Teresa of Calcutta reminded us, "When you look at the Crucifix, you understand how much Jesus loved you then. When you look at the Sacred Host you understand how much Jesus loves you now."

CHAPTER 1

The Tree of Life

"The Lord God planted...the tree of life in the middle of the garden." **Gen 2:8-9**

Opening Prayer

O God, come to my assistance.
O Lord, make haste to help me.

Glory be to the Father
and to the Son
and to the Holy Spirit,
As it was in the beginning,
is now, and ever shall be,
world without end. Amen.

Act of Adoration

I place myself in the presence of Him, in whose Incarnate Presence I am before. I place myself there. I adore You, O my Savior, present here as God and as man, in soul and in body, in true flesh and blood. I acknowledge and confess that I kneel before that Sacred Humanity, which was conceived in Mary's womb, and lay in Mary's bosom; which grew up to twelve, wrought miracles, and spoke words of wisdom and peace; which in due

season hung on the cross, lay in the tomb, rose from the dead, and now reigns in heaven. I praise, and bless, and give myself wholly to Him, who is the true Bread of my soul, and my everlasting joy. *St. John Henry Newman*

Reflection

In the mythologies of the ancient world, the image of a tree of life plays a prominent role. The Egyptians looked to the tree of life as the source of eternal life. However, it belonged to the gods. It was inaccessible to mere mortals. It is otherwise in Sacred Scripture.

When God planted a garden in Eden, He placed in it the tree of life. "The Lord God made all sorts of beautiful and nourishing trees sprout out of the earth, among which was the tree of life in the middle of the garden..." (Gen 2:9). God gave the tree of life a most prominent position. With its view clearly visible and access to it unobstructed, the tree of life assured our first parents that the Creator wanted them to live and to enjoy the happiness for which He created them.

God forbade Adam and Eve to eat of the tree of the knowledge of good and evil. He gave no such prohibition concerning the tree of life. In the Garden of Eden, "man was furnished with food against hunger, with drink against thirst, and with the tree of life against the ravages of old age" (St. Augustine, *City of God*, xiv. 26). "God did not make death nor does he delight in the death of the living" (Wis 1:13).

It was by their disobedience that Adam and Eve came under the curse of death. They became subject to the slow decay of the body and the end of life on earth as a painful and unwelcome reality. Certainly, earthly life would have come to an end. But, eating of the tree of life and living in obedience to God would have made the passage from this world to the next a joy-filled and painless transition.

After Adam and Eve sinned, God cast them out from the garden to prevent them "from reaching out and taking the fruit of the tree of life lest [they] eat it and live forever" (Gen 3:22). From the text, it seems clear that, before their sin of disobedience, Adam and Eve had not yet eaten of the tree of life. Thus, once driven from Eden, they lost the possibility of eating from the tree and gaining immortality.

Denying Adam and Eve access to the tree of life seems like a harsh punishment. But it was not! It was a mercy given to them in their sinful state. "Now that they were clothed in the curse, [God] kept them back from eating of the tree of life, lest by eating of it and living forever, they would have to remain in a life of pain for eternity...The tree of life would have made them entombed all their lives, leaving them forever tortured by their pains" (St. Ephrem the Syrian, *Commentary on Genesis*, Section II, 35).

God had created the tree of life as something good for humankind. Because of original sin, it could no longer achieve its purpose. But God did not change His plan. He made us for life in this world and eternal life with Him in heaven. Therefore, God sent His only-begotten Son to reverse the sin of Adam. "The tree of life which was planted by God in Paradise prefigured this precious Cross. For since death was by a tree, it was fitting that life and resurrection should be bestowed by a tree" (St. John Damascene, *Exposition of the Faith*, Book IV, Chapter 11).

In speaking about Himself as the Good Shepherd who lays down His life for His sheep, Jesus says, "I have come that they may have life, and have it in abundance" (Jn 10:10). By Christ's Death and Resurrection, Jesus frees us from the curse of death. He saves us from eternal death and shares with us God's own life in this world. What the tree of life in the garden merely symbolized, the Cross accomplished on Golgotha. Death no longer has dominion over us. In Christ, we are already gifted with eternal life.

The Cross is the Tree of Life. And hanging upon that tree is Jesus, Body and Blood, Soul and Divinity. The fruit of the tree of life is now the flesh and blood of Jesus given us in the Eucharist. As Jesus Himself says, "Whoever feeds upon my flesh and drinks my blood has eternal life and I will raise him up on the last day" (Jn 6:54).

Adam and Eve forfeited eternal life by eating of the tree of the knowledge of good and evil. We gain eternal life by eating the Eucharist, the fruit of the Cross, the tree of life eternal. The Eucharist is "the medicine of immortality, the antidote we take in order not to die but to live forever in Jesus Christ" (St. Ignatius of Antioch, *Letter to the Ephesians*, 20.2).

As the tree of life stood in the midst of the garden, Jesus in the Eucharist is now in the midst of the Church. He is in our sight and within our reach. He is accessible to us sinners. He beckons us to come to Him. While the other sacraments touch us with the healing power of the Divine Physician, the Eucharist is the Divine Physician Himself.

In the Eucharist, we encounter Jesus who brings comfort to our sorrows, healing to our hurts and, as God wills, a remedy for illness. Before the Eucharist, we are in the presence of Jesus who wills to cast out evil from our hearts and mend our broken bodies. The Eucharist is "the flesh of our savior Jesus Christ, which suffered for our sins and which the Father by His goodness raised up" (St. Ignatius of Antioch, *Letter to the Smyrnaeans*, 7). In the Eucharist, Christ is both physician and medicine. He brings healing to souls, health to our bodies, and the gift of immortality.

St. Francis de Sales once said, "If worldly people ask you why you receive Communion so often, tell them that it is to learn to love God, be purified from imperfections, delivered from misery, comforted in affliction and supported in weakness.... Tell them that two classes of people should communicate frequently: the sick that they may be restored to health and the healthy lest they fall sick" (*Introduction to the Devout Life*, 52).

> *The Fruit of righteousness and the Tree of Life is Christ. He alone, as man, fulfilled all righteousness. And with his own underived life, he has brought forth the fruits of knowledge and virtue like a tree, whereof they that eat shall receive eternal life, and shall enjoy the tree of life in paradise, with Adam and all the righteous.* — *St. Hippolytus of Rome*

Prayer

Restore to me, O Lord, the robe of immortality, which was lost in the transgression of our first parents, and, inasmuch as I approach your Sacred Mysteries in an unworthy manner, nevertheless, may I be made deserving of eternal blessedness.

From the Vesting Prayers for the Priest before Mass

May the heart of Jesus, in the Most Blessed Sacrament, be praised, adored, and loved with grateful affection, at every moment, in all the tabernacles of the world, even to the end of time. Amen.

Additional prayers begin on page 161

CHAPTER 2

Abel the Just

"The Lord was pleased with Abel and his offering." **Gen 4:4**

Opening Prayer

O God, come to my assistance.
O Lord, make haste to help me.

Glory be to the Father
and to the Son
and to the Holy Spirit,
As it was in the beginning,
is now, and ever shall be,
world without end. Amen.

Act of Adoration

I place myself in the presence of Him, in whose Incarnate Presence I am before. I place myself there. I adore You, O my Savior, present here as God and as man, in soul and in body, in true flesh and blood. I acknowledge and confess that I kneel before that Sacred Humanity, which was conceived in Mary's womb, and lay in Mary's bosom; which grew up to twelve, wrought miracles, and spoke words of wisdom and peace; which in due season hung on the cross, lay in the tomb,

rose from the dead, and now reigns in heaven. I praise, and bless, and give myself wholly to Him, who is the true Bread of my soul, and my everlasting joy. *St. John Henry Newman*

Reflection

At the end of his life, Jesus saw His own imminent death as the culmination of a long series of martyrdoms going all the way back to the first murder in the Bible. He denounces those members of His own people whose hypocrisy precipitates His death. He says, "Upon you will fall the guilt of all the innocent blood that has been shed upon the earth, from the blood of the righteous Abel to the blood of Zechariah..." (Mt 23:35).

Jesus calls Abel "righteous." The New Testament Greek word δίκαιος (dikaios) can be translated either as "righteous" or as "just." It means someone who lives in conformity to God's will. Jesus places Abel the Just at the head of a long procession of holy ones persecuted for their godly lives. Abel speaks not a single word in Sacred Scripture. He is martyred for the example of goodness he gave. In the Beatitudes, Jesus Himself declares such a person who suffers for the sake of righteousness (justice) worthy of heaven (Mt 5:10).

Genesis only tells us that Abel made an offering to God from the firstborn of his flock and this pleased God. The Letter to the Hebrews, however, explains the reason why God was pleased. "By faith Abel offered to God a better sacrifice than that of Cain. Because of this, he was attested as righteous, God himself bearing witness to his gifts..." (Heb 11:4). It was the spiritual attitude of Abel's heart that made his offering acceptable in God's sight. Abel's sacrifice, sprinkled with the sweet incense of humble faith, rose acceptable in the sight of God. As our heart, so our offering.

"The Lord was pleased with Abel and his offering but he was not pleased with Cain and his offering" (Gen 4:4-5). Notice the wording of the sacred text. God looked first at the one offering and only then on the gift offered. Abel approached God with humility. As his hands drew the knife to sacrifice his victim, his eyes looked to the heavens from whence came every blessing.

"God had respect to the gifts of Abel, because he offered with single-mindedness and righteousness; but He had no respect unto the offering of Cain, because his heart was divided with envy and malice...It is the conscience of the offerer that sanctifies the sacrifice when it is pure, and thus moves God to accept [the offering] as from a friend." (St. Irenaeus, *Against Heresies*, 4.18.3).

Like Abel, we need to approach the Eucharist with a spirit of righteousness and innocence. It is vain to offer prayers with our lips if our hearts harbor evil. A life of goodness is the first approach to the Divine Presence. Nonetheless, our sins should not deter us from coming to the Lord. Christ is present in the Eucharist, waiting for us, eager to receive our contrite spirit and to heal us. He will never send us away. As the sun bleaches our discolored and stained clothes, the love of Christ in the Eucharist brightens our sin-stained souls with grace and makes all our offerings acceptable. The Eucharist is the steadfast kindness of God to us sinners.

> *Abel, peaceable and righteous in sacrificing in innocence to God, taught the rest of us that when we bring our gift to the altar we should come, like him, with the fear of God, with a heart free of deceit, with the law of righteousness, with the peace of concord. He sacrificed in such a way, and so he was worthy to become, afterwards, himself a sacrifice to God: he who bore witness through the first martyrdom, who initiated the Lord's passion by the glory of his blood, had both the Lord's righteousness and the Lord's peace. Such are those who are crowned by the Lord at the end;*

such are those who will sit and judge with him on the Day of Judgment.

St. Cyprian, On the Lord's Prayer

Prayer

I entreat you, O Lord, by this most holy mystery of your Body and Blood, wherewith we are daily fed, and cleansed, and sanctified in your Church, and are made partakers of the one Supreme Divinity, grant unto me your holy virtues, that filled therewith I may with a good conscience draw near to [you]...

Come into my soul; heal and cleanse me within and without; be the protection and continual health of my soul and body. Drive far from me all foes that lie in wait: let them flee afar off at the presence of your power; that, strengthened by you without and within, I may by a straight way arrive at your kingdom, where, not as now in mysteries, but face to face, we shall behold you...with the Father and the Holy Spirit, forever and ever world without end. Amen. *St. Ambrose*

May the heart of Jesus, in the Most Blessed Sacrament, be praised, adored, and loved with grateful affection, at every moment, in all the tabernacles of the world, even to the end of time. Amen.

Additional prayers begin on page 161

CHAPTER 3

The Sacrifice of Abel

"Cain offered the fruit of the earth as a sacrifice to the Lord, and Abel offered the firstborn of his flock..." **Gen 4:3-4**

Opening Prayer

O God, come to my assistance.
O Lord, make haste to help me.

Glory be to the Father
and to the Son
and to the Holy Spirit,
As it was in the beginning,
is now, and ever shall be,
world without end. Amen.

Act of Adoration

I place myself in the presence of Him, in whose Incarnate Presence I am before. I place myself there. I adore You, O my Savior, present here as God and as man, in soul and in body, in true flesh and blood. I acknowledge and confess that I kneel before that Sacred Humanity, which was conceived in Mary's womb, and lay in Mary's bosom; which grew up to twelve, wrought miracles, and spoke words of wisdom and peace; which in due

season hung on the cross, lay in the tomb, rose from the dead, and now reigns in heaven. I praise, and bless, and give myself wholly to Him, who is the true Bread of my soul, and my everlasting joy. *St. John Henry Newman*

Reflection

When Eve gave birth to Cain, her first child, she exclaimed, "I have obtained a son from the Lord" (Gen 4:1). His name is a word play on the Hebrew word קנה (qanah; to get, obtain, acquire). Eve gratefully recognized that the precious gift of life comes from God Himself. Her heart overflowed with joy. God had not forsaken her. Although Adam and Eve were exiled from Eden and the Tree of Life, in the birth of Cain, God had given them proof that humankind will have a future.

When Eve bore her second son, she named him Abel. Like his brother's name, his name is also a play on words in Hebrew. "Abel" comes from the word הבל (hebel). This word means a breath or vapor which comes and goes away quickly. Like his name, Abel's life was to quickly pass away at the angry hands of his jealous brother Cain.

Both Cain and Abel are the first individuals Sacred Scripture mentions as offering sacrifice to God. "Cain offered the fruit of the earth as a sacrifice to the Lord, and Abel offered the firstborn of his flock and their fat offerings" (Gen 4:3-4). Both brothers offered their sacrifice from the labor of their hands. The offerings expressed their gratitude to God. All that they had, their life, the increase in their wealth and their health, they owed to God. By their sacrifice, they wished to secure His continued blessing.

"The Lord was pleased with Abel and his offering, but he was not pleased with Cain and his offering" (Gen 4:4-5). Genesis does not directly tell us why God accepted Abel's offering and rejected Cain's. But it does imply the reason. Cain offered "the fruit of the earth." He was a farmer and brings to God some of his produce. Abel, however, was a shepherd and brings to God "the firstborn of his flock and their fat offerings."

"Cain brought to God what he had. Abel carefully chose the firstborn. [Abel] did not merely offer sheep, but of the firstborn, that is, of the most precious and the most excellent, and then, of these firstborn the most precious parts, and of their fat, it says that is, of the fattest and the best. Nothing of the sort is recorded of Cain. He offered sacrifice from the fruits of the earth, as though to say, whatever he came across, taking no labor or pains to choose among them" (St. John Chrysostom, *Homilies on Genesis*, 18).

Throughout Scripture, the firstborn is considered special. In the Exodus events, God refers to Israel as His firstborn (Ex 4:22). In the instructions God gives for the celebration of the Passover, He says, "Consecrate each firstborn to me, whatever opens the womb in Israel, whether human or animal; it belongs to me" (Ex 13:2). The firstborn is more precious because it holds the promise of the future. Abel offered the best of what he possessed.

Abel's sacrifice is the Old Testament's first recorded sacrifice of a lamb from the firstborn of his flock. It prefigures the Eucharist. The Eucharist is Jesus, "the firstborn of creation" (Col 1:15). He is the "Lamb without blemish or defect…chosen before the foundation of the world" (1 Pet 1:19-20). The Eucharist is Jesus the Lamb slain from the foundation of the world (Rev 13:8).

Abel was a shepherd who offered a lamb. Jesus is the Good Shepherd. He offers Himself. He is the "Lamb of God who takes away the sin of the world" (Jn 1:29). The Eucharist is Jesus offering to the Father what is worth more than all creation.

Coming before the Eucharist, like Abel, we bring our earnest desire for God's blessing. We come to offer all that we do by uniting ourselves with Jesus. We are not prodigal in what we lavish upon God. He deserves the best. We give Him the choice moments of our day. When we come to Him when we tend to be less distracted, He is most pleased.

The Eucharist is the abiding sign of God's infinite generosity. When we come before the love of God poured out in Jesus, God does not hold back pouring out His goodness on us, our families and on our world. Whatever we sacrifice for His honor, we receive back a hundredfold. United with Christ in the Eucharist, we ourselves become "a sacrificial offering whose fragrance is pleasing to God" (Eph 5:2).

> *The Church and the world have a great need of Eucharistic worship. Jesus waits for us in this Sacrament of Love. Let us be generous with our time in going to meet Him in adoration and in contemplation that is full of faith and ready to make reparation for the great faults and crimes of the world. May our adoration never cease.*
>
> *Pope St. John Paul II,*
> *Dominicae Cenae, 3*

Prayer

Jesus, Victim, I want to comfort you.
I unite myself with you.
I offer myself in union with you....
Take me. I give myself to you.

I entrust to you all my actions
and thoughts —
my mind, that you may enlighten it,
my heart, that you may fill it,
my will, that you may establish it,
my soul and body,
that you may feed and sustain them.
Eucharistic Heart of Jesus,
Whose Blood is the life of my soul,
may it no longer be I who live,
but you alone who lives in me. Amen.

May the heart of Jesus, in the Most Blessed Sacrament, be praised, adored, and loved with grateful affection, at every moment, in all the tabernacles of the world, even to the end of time. Amen.

Additional prayers begin on page 161

CHAPTER 4

The Blood of Abel

"Your brother's blood cries out to me from the soil." **Gen 4:10**

Opening Prayer

O God, come to my assistance.
O Lord, make haste to help me.

Glory be to the Father
and to the Son
and to the Holy Spirit,
As it was in the beginning,
is now, and ever shall be,
world without end. Amen.

Act of Adoration

I place myself in the presence of Him, in whose Incarnate Presence I am before. I place myself there. I adore You, O my Savior, present here as God and as man, in soul and in body, in true flesh and blood. I acknowledge and confess that I kneel before that Sacred Humanity, which was conceived in Mary's womb, and lay in Mary's bosom; which grew up to twelve, wrought miracles, and spoke words of wisdom and peace; which in due season hung on the cross, lay in the tomb,

rose from the dead, and now reigns in heaven. I praise, and bless, and give myself wholly to Him, who is the true Bread of my soul, and my everlasting joy. *St. John Henry Newman*

Reflection

Nicholas of Lyra was one of the most influential medieval biblical commentators. His commentary on Genesis and Exodus contains a highly significant illustration. Adam is working the soil. He smiles at Eve who is holding Abel on her lap. The child affectionately presses his face against his mother's. This image of Eve and Abel strongly resembles the many paintings of the Madonna and the child Jesus from the Middle Ages.

By picturing Eve seated like the Madonna caressing her son, the manuscript illustrator is telling us that Mary is the Second Eve. "The knot of Eve's disobedience was untied by Mary's obedience. What Eve bound through her unbelief, Mary loosed by her faith" (St. Irenaeus, *Against Heresies*, 4). And, the illustrator is also telling us that Jesus is prefigured by Abel. What Abel did, Jesus brought to completion.

The innocent Abel was pleasing to God. Jesus was the Sinless One, in whom the Father was well pleased (Mt 3:17). When God accepted Abel's sacrifice and not Cain's, Cain became filled with envy and killed his brother. Just as Abel was murdered by a wicked brother, Jesus was crucified at the hands of His wicked brethren. Abel's death was the shedding of innocent blood. So too Jesus' death on the Cross. In mingling his own blood with that of the lamb he sacrificed, Abel prefigures Jesus, who is both priest and victim.

God called Cain to a swift accounting for his sin. "Nothing in creation is hidden from [God's] sight. Everything is uncovered and exposed to the eyes of the one to whom we must all render an account" (Heb 4:13). With the very same words He used to question Eve after her sin, God asks Cain, "What have you done?" (Gen 4:10). Cain could lie but he could not hide his crime. Abel's blood testified to his crime and accused him. God said to Cain, "Your brother's blood cries out to me from the soil" (Gen 4:10).

The New Testament sees the blood of Abel as prefiguring the blood of Christ. The Letter to the Hebrews tell us that Jesus is "the mediator of a new covenant" and His "sprinkled blood...speaks more powerfully than even the blood of Abel" (Heb 12:24). "The blood of Abel cried for vengeance; that of Christ for remission" (Erasmus). The blood of Abel cried out to the ears of God for justice. Jesus' blood pleads directly to the heart of God for mercy.

In the sacrifices of the Old Testament, the shedding of blood signified atonement (Lev 17:11). The sins of God's people were covered over by sprinkling the blood of the sacrifice on the mercy-seat in the Holy of Holies. Jesus did not cover over our sins. By shedding His blood on the Cross, He washed them away. In the Old Testament, the blood of the sacrificial victim had to be poured out entirely. By the intense suffering and death Jesus endured, He poured out His entire blood for us. He gave His life totally for our salvation.

Jesus who shed His blood on the Cross and rose from the dead is not bound by time and space. He is truly present to us in the Sacrament of the Altar. And so, in coming before the Eucharist, we come before Jesus, body and blood, soul and divinity. We are with Jesus who ransoms us from our sinful past "not with perishable things like silver or gold, but with the precious blood of Christ..." (1 Pet 1:18).

His precious blood that flowed from His pierced heart continues to cover us. "The blood of ...Jesus... purifies us from all sin" (1 Jn 1:7). His blood cries out to God, "Father, forgive them" (Lk 23:34). What love that knows no limits to make us holy and pleasing to God!

The blood of Jesus calls out more eloquently than Abel's, for the blood of Abel asked for the death of Cain, the fratricide, while the blood of the Lord has asked for, and obtained, life for his persecutors.

If the sacrament of the Lord's passion is to work its effect in us, we must imitate what we receive and proclaim to mankind what we revere. The cry of the Lord finds a hiding place in us if our lips fail to speak of this, though our hearts believe in it. So that his cry may not lie concealed in us it remains for us all, each in his own measure, to make known to those around us the mystery of our new life in Christ.

St. Gregory the Great, Moral Reflections on Job, Lib. 13, 21-23

Prayer

Litany of the Precious Blood

Lord, have mercy on us.
Christ, have mercy on us.
Lord, have mercy on us. Christ, hear us.
Christ, graciously hear us.

God, the Father of Heaven, *have mercy on us.*
God the Son, Redeemer of the world, *have mercy on us.*
God, the Holy Spirit, *have mercy on us.*
Holy Trinity, One God, *have mercy on us.*

Blood of Christ, only-begotten Son
of the Eternal Father, *save us.* (after each line)
Blood of Christ, Incarnate Word of God,
Blood of Christ, of the New and Eternal Testament,
Blood of Christ, falling upon the earth in the Agony,
Blood of Christ, shed profusely in the Scourging,
Blood of Christ, flowing forth in the Crowning with Thorns,
Blood of Christ, poured out on the Cross,
Blood of Christ, price of our salvation,
Blood of Christ, without which there is no forgiveness,
Blood of Christ, Eucharistic drink and refreshment of souls,
Blood of Christ, stream of mercy,
Blood of Christ, victor over demons,
Blood of Christ, courage of martyrs,
Blood of Christ, strength of confessors,
Blood of Christ, bringing forth virgins,
Blood of Christ, help of those in peril,
Blood of Christ, relief of the burdened,
Blood of Christ, solace in sorrow,
Blood of Christ, hope of the penitent,
Blood of Christ, consolation of the dying,
Blood of Christ, peace and tenderness of hearts,

Blood of Christ, pledge of Eternal Life,
Blood of Christ, freeing souls from purgatory,
Blood of Christ, most worthy of all glory and honor,

Lamb of God, Who takes away the sins of the world,
Spare us, O Lord.
Lamb of God, Who takes away the sins of the world,
Graciously hear us, O Lord.
Lamb of God, Who takes away the sins of the world,
Have mercy on us.

℣. Thou hast redeemed us, O Lord, in Thy Blood.
℟. And made us, for our God, a kingdom.

Prayer

Almighty and eternal God, Thou hast appointed Thine only-begotten Son the Redeemer of the world and willed to be appeased by his blood. Grant, we beg of Thee, that we may worthily adore this price of our salvation and through its power be safeguarded from the evils of the present life so that we may rejoice in its fruits forever in heaven. Through the same Christ our Lord. Amen.

May the heart of Jesus, in the Most Blessed Sacrament, be praised, adored, and loved with grateful affection, at every moment, in all the tabernacles of the world, even to the end of time. Amen.

Additional prayers begin on page 161

CHAPTER 5

Melchizedek

"Melchizedek, the king of Salem, offered bread and wine...and blessed Abram."

Gen 14:18-19

Opening Prayer

O God, come to my assistance.
O Lord, make haste to help me.

Glory be to the Father
and to the Son
and to the Holy Spirit,
As it was in the beginning,
is now, and ever shall be,
world without end. Amen.

Act of Adoration

I place myself in the presence of Him, in whose Incarnate Presence I am before. I place myself there. I adore You, O my Savior, present here as God and as man, in soul and in body, in true flesh and blood. I acknowledge and confess that I kneel before that Sacred Humanity, which was conceived in Mary's womb, and lay in Mary's bosom; which grew up to twelve, wrought miracles, and spoke words of wisdom and peace; which in due

season hung on the cross, lay in the tomb, rose from the dead, and now reigns in heaven. I praise, and bless, and give myself wholly to Him, who is the true Bread of my soul, and my everlasting joy. *St. John Henry Newman*

Reflection

After the first war recorded in Sacred Scripture, the mysterious figure of Melchizedek makes a brief appearance. Four kings from the region of Mesopotamia had come to wage war with five kings living close to Abraham in the Promised Land. When these kings took Abraham's nephew Lot captive, Abraham joined the battle against them. A good example. In times of distress, we need to do all we can to keep our families united. When our relatives are in a difficult situation, our hand should reach out to help them.

While those kings who had attacked Abraham's neighbors were enjoying the spoils of war, Abraham completely surprised them. He attacked them at night with his small force of fresh troops. They fled in terror and Abraham returned home victorious.

At this point, Melchizedek comes out to meet Abraham. As "a priest of God Most High" (Gen 14:18), he takes precedence over Abraham. Abraham willingly bows his head before this priest to receive his blessing. He is not ashamed to make his dependence on God public. He did not hide his faith. He unfurled his faith like a flag in the wind for all to see.

Melchizedek praises God for granting victory to his chosen servant. By his prayer, he directs Abraham's thoughts away from establishing an earthly kingdom based on military might. Abraham is to depend on God's blessing to keep his family safe as the Chosen People.

Melchizedek, the first priest mentioned in the Scriptures, foreshadows Jesus. The New Testament sees Melchizedek as a figure of Christ our High Priest (Heb 5:6-10; 6:20—7:17). And, the Early Fathers of the Church were quick to see in Melchizedek's offering of bread and wine a prototype of the Eucharist. St. Clement of Alexandria wrote, "Melchizedek, king of Salem, priest of the Most High God ... gave bread and wine, furnishing consecrated food for a type of the Eucharist... " (*Stromata*, Book IV, Chapter 25). St. Cyprian of Carthage likewise taught, "In the priest Melchizedek we see the Sacrament of the Sacrifice of the Lord prefigured" (*Epistle* 62, 4).

In celebrating Mass today, the Church continues to see the king-priest Melchizedek's offering of bread and wine as prefiguring the Eucharist. In the First Eucharistic Prayer after the consecration, the priest prays, "Be pleased to look upon these offerings with a serene and kindly countenance, and to accept them, as you were pleased to accept... the offering of your high priest Melchizedek, a holy sacrifice, a spotless victim." As Melchizedek offered bread and wine to Abraham, Jesus at the Last Supper offered Himself under the form of bread and wine to His apostles.

Melchizedek offered bread and wine to refresh Abraham and his men weary from their long battle. Jesus, the true and eternal High Priest offers Himself to us under the appearances of bread and wine to refresh us in our daily struggle against sin and temptation. In the fourth-century Eucharistic Prayer found in the *Apostolic Constitutions*, the priest prays that those who receive the Eucharist "be delivered from the devil and his deceit."

When we receive the Eucharist and when we adore this Most Blessed Sacrament, Christ floods our souls with His grace. He strengthens our will and weakens the power of concupiscence. The Council of Trent called the Eucharist "an antidote, whereby we may be freed from daily faults and be preserved from mortal sins" (Session XIII, 11 October 1551, "Decree on the Most Holy Eucharist," Chapter 2).

St. Cyril of Alexandria, one of the greatest defenders of the divinity of Jesus, recognized the power of the Eucharist to help us in our struggle to follow Christ each day. His words encouraging us to come to Jesus in the Eucharist are as relevant today as they were when he penned them in the 5th century.

> *If the poison of pride is swelling up in you, turn to the Eucharist; and that Bread, which is your God humbling and disguising himself, will teach you humility. If the fever of selfish greed rages in you, feed on this Bread; and you will learn generosity. If the cold wind of coveting withers you, hasten to the Bread of Angels; and charity will come to blossom in your heart. If you feel the itch of intemperance, nourish yourself with the flesh and blood of Christ, who practiced heroic self-control during his earthly life; and you will become temperate. If you are lazy and sluggish about spiritual things, strengthen yourself with this heavenly food; and you will grow fervent. Lastly, if you feel scorched by the fever of impurity, go to the banquet of the angels; and the spotless flesh of Christ will make you pure and chaste*
>
> *St. Cyril of Alexandria*

The chaos of the world and the cares of everyday life can easily weary us and tempt us to abandon the good fight. Personal misfortunes, sickness, and misunderstandings darken all our paths. And we lose hope. We need the strength to uphold the gospel and the courage to stand for our basic moral values in today's world. In the Eucharist, we find that strength and fortitude.

Long before His birth as the Messiah, the prophet Isaiah called Jesus "Mighty God" (Isa 9:5). The Hebrew word גבור (gibbor: mighty) implies someone who has fought a battle and is victorious. The word conjures up the image of a man fighting with all his vigor, being injured in the battle, but winning the crown of victory. Jesus who went to the Cross and was bruised for our offenses has won the battle over evil. He is truly our "Mighty God" present before us in the Eucharist and continually sustaining us in the struggles of this life.

> *Only through the Eucharist is it possible to live the heroic virtues of Christianity: charity, to the point of forgiving one's enemies; love for those who make us suffer; chastity in every age and situation of life; patience in suffering and when one is shocked by the silence of God in the tragedies of history or of one's own personal existence. You must always be Eucharistic souls in order to be authentic Christians.*
>
> *Pope St. John Paul II*

Prayer

Soul of Christ, sanctify me.
Body of Christ, save me.
Blood of Christ, inebriate me.
Water from the side of Christ, wash me.
Passion of Christ, strengthen me.
O Good Jesus, hear me.
Within Thy wounds hide me.
Suffer me not to be separated from Thee.
From the malignant enemy defend me.
In the hour of my death call me.
And bid me come unto Thee,
That with all Thy saints,
I may praise Thee
Forever and ever. Amen.

St. Ignatius of Loyola

May the heart of Jesus, in the Most Blessed Sacrament, be praised, adored, and loved with grateful affection, at every moment, in all the tabernacles of the world, even to the end of time. Amen.

Additional prayers begin on page 161

CHAPTER 6

Moriah and Golgotha

"They set out together." **Gen 22:6**

Opening Prayer

O God, come to my assistance.
O Lord, make haste to help me.

Glory be to the Father
and to the Son
and to the Holy Spirit,
As it was in the beginning,
is now, and ever shall be,
world without end. Amen.

Act of Adoration

I place myself in the presence of Him, in whose Incarnate Presence I am before. I place myself there. I adore You, O my Savior, present here as God and as man, in soul and in body, in true flesh and blood. I acknowledge and confess that I kneel before that Sacred Humanity, which was conceived in Mary's womb, and lay in Mary's bosom; which grew up to twelve, wrought miracles, and spoke words of wisdom and peace; which in due season hung on the cross, lay in the tomb,

rose from the dead, and now reigns in heaven. I praise, and bless, and give myself wholly to Him, who is the true Bread of my soul, and my everlasting joy. *St. John Henry Newman*

Reflection

Archaeologists digging through layers of civilization in the Holy Land have unearthed the charred bodies of infants at such strategic sites as Megiddo, Ta'anach, and Gezer. From North Mesopotamian texts dating from the 10th through the 7th century, we know that Israel's pagan neighbors offered their sons as burnt offering to their gods. The Torah clearly condemns such a barbaric custom as a most egregious sin (Lev 20:2; Deut 12:31). But the fact that the prophets Jeremiah and Ezekiel hurl fierce denunciations against child sacrifice (Jer 7:30-32; 19:3-5; Ezek 16:20-21) may indicate the Israelites did the same.

Child sacrifice as a religious ritual truly shocks us. Even at a time when so many condone the sacrifice of the child in the womb on the altar of personal choice, we find this religious custom abhorrent. Thus, when we read the account of Abraham's sacrifice of Isaac, we begin to wonder. Could the command for Abraham to offer up Isaac really have come from God? Or is it possible that the idea came from Abraham's own imperfect understanding of God in light of the religious practices of his day?

The command of God to sacrifice the son of the promise would not have struck Abraham as inherently immoral. God has absolute dominion over all life. But as the narrative makes clear, God chose to lead Abraham to Mt. Moriah not to slay his son but to enlighten his conscience. Like a wise surgeon, he exposed the evil in human society to cure it.

God is a wise teacher. He gradually leads humanity to a deeper understanding of His will. The conclusion in the story of Abraham's sacrifice of Isaac is the point of the narrative. To the God of life, the sacrifice of a son is abhorrent. It does not wring from His clenched fist a blessing on the father and his family. Certainly, we must hold all other loves in our lives as less than love of God. We must be ready to sacrifice what is dearest to us if it holds us back from loving God above all. But God does not require nor does He want child sacrifice.

Abraham had to travel three days with Isaac to the place of sacrifice. With each step, Abraham foresaw years of suffering, of waiting for a son, painfully vanishing in the smoke of sacrifice. In the ruddy face of his beloved son, he beheld the cold pallor of death. But it was from all eternity that God saw the face of

His Son drained of all life on the Cross and yet He willed it for our salvation. Abraham had prepared for three days. God had prepared for the sacrifice of His Son from the very hour Adam and Eve sinned. All of sacred history was leading to Golgotha.

God clearly indicates to Abraham the place of sacrifice as Mt. Moriah. The author of Chronicles tells us that this is the place in Jerusalem where Solomon built the Temple (2 Chr 3:1). According to tradition, it is also the place where Jesus, the Beloved Son of the Father, gave His life in sacrifice for our sins and became the foundation stone (λίθος: *lithos*) of the New Temple, not built by hands, but of living stones (1 Pet 2:4-5). Jesus Christ is a carefully chosen and hewn stone (λίθος: *lithos*), specially laid as the first in the work of building that we continue with our lives.

To the place of sacrifice, Abraham and Isaac "set out together" (Gen 22:6). So also God the Father and His Son Jesus went together to Golgotha. They were one in redeeming us. "Amen, amen, I say to you, the Son can do nothing by himself; he can do only what he sees the Father doing. For whatever the Father does, the Son also does" (Jn 5:19).

The Father was with the Son for the whole of His earthly ministry. He was with Him until the end when the Son "gave himself for our sins...in accordance with the will of our God and Father" (Gal 1:4). The Father was not absent from Golgotha. He was there, not at a distance, but close at hand, offering up His Son for us. "For God so loved the world, that he gave his only Son so that everyone who believes in him may not perish, but may attain eternal life" (Jn 3:16).

After Abraham sacrificed the ram that God provided in place of Isaac, Abraham named the place "The Lord will provide" (Gen 22:14). He speaks of the future, even though God had already provided the ram for the sacrifice. Prophetically, he is pointing to Christ, the sacrificial victim whom the Father will provide on Golgotha.

The very same Hebrew words that are translated "The Lord will provide" can also be translated "God shall be seen." In the death of Christ on the Cross, we come to see God in a way we would never know Him on our own. We see Him as lavishing His love on us beyond all measure. Christ died for us because God loves us. "He did not spare his own Son but handed him over for all of us. How then can he fail... to give us everything else along with him?" (Rom 8:32).

In the Eucharist, the Father is still providing for all our needs. Strength for our weakness. Light for our blindness. Zeal for our indifference. Wisdom for our folly. Forgiveness for our sins. In this great Sacrament, the Father offers us His own Beloved Son to be with us and to accompany us every step of our lives. He joins us to Jesus, giving us eternal life and forming us into the New Temple where we offer the spiritual worship of our lives.

> *The Father of all wished his Christ take upon himself the curses of the whole human family, knowing that, after he had been crucified and was dead, he would raise him up. . . . His Father wished him to suffer this, in order that by his stripes the human race might be healed.*
>
> *Justin Martyr,*
> *Dialogue with Trypho, 95*

Prayer

All glory and praise to you, Almighty Father:
in your tender mercy you so loved the world
that you gave up your Beloved Son to die for us on the Cross.
In the great Sacrament of the Eucharist,
we ascend the hill of Golgotha to be united with him.

Grant us who venerate and adore the Most Blessed Sacrament a fresh outpouring of your Holy Spirit,
the forgiveness of all our sins
and all that we need to do your Holy Will.
Through Christ our Lord. Amen.

May the heart of Jesus, in the Most Blessed Sacrament, be praised, adored, and loved with grateful affection, at every moment, in all the tabernacles of the world, even to the end of time. Amen.

Additional prayers begin on page 161

CHAPTER 7

The Sacrifice of Isaac

"Take your son, your only son, the one you love, Isaac and...offer him as a burnt offering..." Gen 22:2

Opening Prayer

O God, come to my assistance.
O Lord, make haste to help me.

Glory be to the Father
and to the Son
and to the Holy Spirit,
As it was in the beginning,
is now, and ever shall be,
world without end. Amen.

Act of Adoration

I place myself in the presence of Him, in whose Incarnate Presence I am before. I place myself there. I adore You, O my Savior, present here as God and as man, in soul and in body, in true flesh and blood. I acknowledge and confess that I kneel before that Sacred Humanity, which was conceived in Mary's womb, and lay in Mary's bosom; which grew up to twelve, wrought miracles, and spoke words of wisdom and peace; which in due

season hung on the cross, lay in the tomb, rose from the dead, and now reigns in heaven. I praise, and bless, and give myself wholly to Him, who is the true Bread of my soul, and my everlasting joy. *St. John Henry Newman*

Reflection

When the Christians of the first few centuries decorated the catacombs, they gave primary importance to the Eucharist. One famous fresco of the Eucharist is found in Rome's Catacombs of St. Callixtus. It not only shows Christians celebrating the Eucharist, but it also depicts Abraham sacrificing his son Isaac. Christians saw that Old Testament event as pointing to the Eucharist.

In his very person, Isaac foreshadowed Jesus. In His birth, God intervened in a special way. Abraham was one hundred years old and Sarah ninety when Isaac was born. Even more special was God's intervention in the birth of Jesus. By the overshadowing of the Holy Spirit, God overcame not the age of Mary, but her virginity. Isaac is Abraham's only son, his beloved son whom he loves (Gen 22:2). Jesus is God's only Son, His beloved Son (Mk 1:11). Both Isaac and Jesus embody God's promise of blessing and salvation.

In Genesis 22:2-18, God tells Abraham to sacrifice his beloved son as a burnt offering.

The biblical narrator records this event with chaste simplicity. There is nothing in the Old Testament more touching than the pathos of this Old Testament event. Isaac is curious. He innocently asks his father, "Here are the fire and the wood, but where is the lamb for the burnt offering?" (Gen 22:7). With self-restraint and calm faith, Abraham responds, "God himself will provide the lamb for the burning offering, my son" (Gen 22:8).

The narrator gives no analysis of the deep emotion stirring in the heart of Abraham. He spares not a single word about the apprehension gripping Isaac. The visible facts: that is all he gives us. God speaks and Abraham obeys. Abraham speaks and Isaac obeys.

For three days, Abraham and Isaac travel to the land of Moriah. This is the place God designated for the sacrifice of Isaac. They build an altar. Abraham binds Isaac and places him on the firewood.

From Isaac, not even a sigh of protest. Just total acquiescence to the will of his father. According to the first century Jewish historian Flavius Josephus, Isaac, knowing that he is the victim, willingly rushes to the altar. He is a prototype of Jesus Himself who said, "No one takes [my life] from me. I lay it down of my own free will" (Jn 10:18).

The very moment, Abraham raises his hand to slay his beloved son, an angel calls out to him, "Abraham, Abraham... do not reach out your hand against the boy! Do not harm him in any way! Abraham looked up and saw a ram that had its horns caught in a bush. Abraham took the ram and offered it as a burnt offering instead of his son" (Gen 22:11-13). God did provide as Abraham had prophesied.

Christian tradition, even from New Testament times, has read this Old Testament event, as a foreshadowing of the sacrifice of the Cross. Isaac carries on his shoulders the wood of sacrifice just as Jesus carried the wood of the Cross. Isaac was bound and placed on the altar. Jesus was bound and nailed to the Cross. Both Isaac and Jesus willingly accepted their father's will and surrender themselves to death. For three days, Isaac was as good as dead. For three days, Jesus was truly dead and laid in a tomb. After three days, Isaac was returned to his father alive. On the third day, Jesus rose from the dead.

Isaac was saved from being sacrificed because God Himself provided a ram. In ancient times, the ram was a symbol for the king. Many of the Fathers of the Church saw in the ram caught by its horns in the thicket a foreshadowing of Christ who was crowned with thorns and who became the King of all nations. God provided a substitute for Isaac about to die so that he might live. God provided Jesus as the one who died in our place on the Cross so that we might have eternal life.

"[God] made him who did not know sin to be sin for our sake, so that through him we might become the righteousness of God" (2 Cor 5:21). By the sacrifice of the Cross, Jesus became sin in the sense that He was the sin-offering that wiped away our sins. His total obedience to the Father on the Cross pierced the heart of God, flooding the world with God's grace.

What the sacrifice of Isaac faintly symbolized, Christ accomplished on Calvary. Jesus who died as the true sacrifice for our sins remains present to us in the Blessed Sacrament. He stays in our midst, patiently, lovingly surrounding us with God's grace. How great His mercy! How strong His example to bear patiently with the trials of this life! How powerful the ideal He sets before us of complete obedience to the will of God.

> *[Jesus] carried the wood on his shoulder as he was led up to be slain like Isaac by his Father, but Christ suffered, whereas Isaac did not suffer; for he was a model of the Christ who was going to suffer. But by being merely the model of Christ he caused astonishment and fear among men. For it was a strange*

mystery to behold, a son led by his father to a mountain for slaughter... But Isaac was silent, ... he carried with fortitude the model of the Lord...On behalf of Isaac the righteous one, a ram appeared for slaughter, so that Isaac might be released from bonds. That ram, slain, ransomed Isaac; so also the Lord, slain, saved us, and sacrificed, ransomed us.

Melitis of Sardis,
On Pascha, Fragment 9-10

Prayer

O God, who crushed the pride of the enemy by the long-suffering of Your Only-begotten Son: grant, we beseech you, that we may worthily recall those things which in His tender love He bore for us; and, thus following His example, may we patiently endure all our adversities. Through the same Christ our Lord. Amen.

May the heart of Jesus, in the Most Blessed Sacrament, be praised, adored, and loved with grateful affection, at every moment, in all the tabernacles of the world, even to the end of time. Amen.

Additional prayers begin on page 161

CHAPTER 8

The Passover Lamb

"Blessed…those…invited to the wedding banquet of the Lamb." **Rev 19:9**

Opening Prayer

O God, come to my assistance.
O Lord, make haste to help me.

Glory be to the Father
and to the Son
and to the Holy Spirit,
As it was in the beginning,
is now, and ever shall be,
world without end. Amen.

Act of Adoration

I place myself in the presence of Him, in whose Incarnate Presence I am before. I place myself there. I adore You, O my Savior, present here as God and as man, in soul and in body, in true flesh and blood. I acknowledge and confess that I kneel before that Sacred Humanity, which was conceived in Mary's womb, and lay in Mary's bosom; which grew up to twelve, wrought miracles, and spoke words of wisdom and peace; which in due season hung on the cross, lay in the tomb,

rose from the dead, and now reigns in heaven. I praise, and bless, and give myself wholly to Him, who is the true Bread of my soul, and my everlasting joy. *St. John Henry Newman*

Reflection

The first century witnessed an unprecedented outburst of Messianic expectation. Rome held sway over the Jewish homeland. These pagan foreigners oppressed the Jews. They exacted heavy tribute to support the state. They populated the land with their idols and looked down on God's Chosen People. Steeped in the biblical tradition, pious Jews living at this time were thoroughly convinced that this was the moment God would send them a savior.

The Jews were anxiously awaiting the Messiah, a descendant of the House of David, to come forward as a military leader. They expected him to be the Lion of Judah, strong and mighty as described by Jacob (Gen 49:8-12). With heroic prowess, he would drive out the Romans and restore Israel's ancient glory.

No one ever thought that the Lion of Judah would be a lamb. They expected their Messiah to slay their enemies. They never dreamed that their enemies would slay their Messiah. How often we need to recall what God says through the prophet Isaiah: "My thoughts are not your thoughts, nor are your ways my ways..." (Isa 55:8).

The crowds came to John the Baptist, hoping he was the Messiah. The fire of his words ignited their Messianic expectation. But John pointed to Jesus and told them, "Behold, the Lamb of God who takes away the sin of the world" (Jn 1:29). The Messiah had come not for the political liberation of one nation, but for the spiritual freedom of all people. John even directed two of his own disciples to leave him and follow Jesus, saying "Behold, the Lamb of God" (Jn 1:36).

The night God delivered the Hebrews from bondage in Egypt, he instituted the Passover. At the center of this rite was the Passover lamb. Each family had to slaughter a one-year-old, unblemished male lamb. They had to spread its blood on the door posts and lintel of their house. And, then, with unleavened bread and bitter herbs, eat the lamb, roasted whole, with not a bone broken.

While the Israelites were safe within their homes, doing as God commanded, the Angel of Death passed over them. The angel dealt death to the firstborn of the Egyptians, forcing Pharaoh's hand. Finally, Pharaoh let the Israelites go. After celebrating the first Passover, they fled Egypt on their long and arduous journey from slavery to freedom.

In the last week of His life, as Jesus entered Jerusalem during the Passover celebrations, shepherds from the nearby hillsides were leading their sheep into the Holy City. From the 10th of Nisan until the day of sacrifice on the 14th, the priests would examine these sheep and certify that they could be bought and offered in sacrifice. It is no mere accident that Jesus chooses to enter Jerusalem at this time. He was the spotless lamb prepared by the Father from the foundation of the world to be offered in sacrifice for our sins (1 Pet 1:19-20).

At the beginning of his gospel, John the Baptist gives Jesus the title "the Lamb of God." At the end of his Gospel, the evangelist indicates how Jesus truly is "the Lamb of God" who accomplishes what the Passover lamb only foreshadowed. According to the fourth gospel, Jesus died on the Cross at the ninth hour, i.e. 3:00 PM, at the very moment the Passover lambs were being killed. Jesus dies on the altar of the Cross as the pure, unblemished lamb not stained by sin (Jn 19:4-8). In the Gospel of Luke, Pilate proclaims Jesus' innocence three times (Lk 23:4,14, 22).

To hasten the death of the crucified, the Roman soldiers would break their legs. But when the soldiers came to Jesus, He was already dead. To make sure He was truly dead, they thrust a lance through His heart (Jn 19:34), thus fulfilling the Scripture that says not a bone of the Paschal lamb could be broken (Ex 12:46). From the pierced heart of Jesus, there flowed out blood and water (Jn 19:34). Christ's death is the birth of the Church. "Water and blood symbolize Baptism and the Holy Eucharist. From these two sacraments the Church is born" (St. John Chrysostom, Cat. 3:13-19).

In the Book of Revelation, the author gives us a glimpse of the Church born on Calvary finally come to glory. Jesus, the Lamb of God, has conquered all the powers of evil. The final victory is His. This is the moment to consummate His marriage with His Bride, the Church. The heavenly multitude breaks into song. Death cannot dissolve this union of Christ and the Church. Gladness fills the hearts of the glorified who hear the angel say, "Blessed are those who are invited to the wedding banquet of the Lamb" (Rev 19:9).

At every Eucharist, the priest invites us to Holy Communion by repeating the words of the angel together with those of John the Baptist: "Behold the Lamb of God, behold him who takes away the sins of the world. Blessed are those called to the supper of the Lamb." For, at every Mass, we are already seated at the marriage feast of the Lamb. At every Eucharist Jesus deepens our union with Him, sharing with us even now the joy of heaven.

When we come before the Blessed Sacrament, we look to the Lamb who suffered, died, and rose for our salvation. We offer Him our own hearts. In the Exodus events, after God laid down all the ways to celebrate the Passover, "the people knelt down and worshiped" (Ex 12:27). We kneel in adoration and worship before so great a Presence, thanking Him that we have passed from death to life and are members of the Church.

> *This is an aspect of the Eucharist which merits greater attention: in celebrating the sacrifice of the Lamb, we are united to the heavenly 'liturgy' and become part of that great multitude which cries out: 'Salvation belongs to our God who sits upon the throne, and to the Lamb!' (Rev 7:10). The Eucharist is truly a glimpse of heaven appearing on earth. It is a glorious ray of the heavenly Jerusalem which pierces the clouds of our history and lights up our journey.*
>
> *Pope St. John Paul II,*
> *Ecclesia de Eucharistia, 19*

Prayer

Worthy is the Lamb that was sacrificed to receive power and riches, wisdom and strength, honor and glory and praise…

To the one seated on the throne and to the Lamb be blessing and honor and glory and might forever and ever.

The reign of the Lord our God, the Almighty, has begun.
Let us rejoice and be glad and give him glory.

For the wedding day of the Lamb has come and the bride has made herself ready.

Rev 5:12-13; 19:6-7

May the heart of Jesus, in the Most Blessed Sacrament, be praised, adored, and loved with grateful affection, at every moment, in all the tabernacles of the world, even to the end of time. Amen.

Additional prayers begin on page 161

CHAPTER 9

Manna for the Journey

The Lord said to Moses, "Behold, I am about to rain bread down from heavens for you." **Ex 16:4**

Opening Prayer

O God, come to my assistance.
O Lord, make haste to help me.

Glory be to the Father
and to the Son
and to the Holy Spirit,
As it was in the beginning,
is now, and ever shall be,
world without end. Amen.

Act of Adoration

I place myself in the presence of Him, in whose Incarnate Presence I am before. I place myself there. I adore You, O my Savior, present here as God and as man, in soul and in body, in true flesh and blood. I acknowledge and confess that I kneel before that Sacred Humanity, which was conceived in Mary's womb, and lay in Mary's bosom; which grew up to twelve, wrought miracles, and spoke

words of wisdom and peace; which in due season hung on the cross, lay in the tomb, rose from the dead, and now reigns in heaven. I praise, and bless, and give myself wholly to Him, who is the true Bread of my soul, and my everlasting joy. *St. John Henry Newman*

Reflection

When God freed the Hebrews from slavery in Egypt, they began their arduous journey to the Promised Land. While in Egypt, they had cried under the cruel oppression of the Pharaoh. They trusted God and He delivered them. But their trust in God was soon tested after they left Egypt. True freedom is only gained in constant obedience to God.

After traveling for one month and a half, the supply of grain which the Hebrews had hastily taken in their flight from Egypt was exhausted. And so were they! Wearied from their wandering in the wilderness, they began to murmur against Moses and Aaron: "Would that the hand of the Lord had killed us in the land of Egypt where we were seated by our pots filled with meat and where we had more than enough bread to eat. Instead you brought us out into this desert to slay the whole assembly with hunger" (Ex 16:3).

How ungrateful! The memory of their miraculous passage through the Red Sea had faded beneath the scorching desert sun. They were ready to bend their back again to oppression just to have a full stomach. They were willing to trade the precious gift of freedom for a few scraps of food. Losing sight of God's providence, they wished that they had died a sudden death at the hand of Pharaoh rather than face the prospect of a long, lingering death at the hand of Moses. More than food, they needed hope.

Seeing their distress, God wasted no time to answer their complaints. God's mercy is never exhausted by our lack of trust. The farther we wander from Him, the greater His effort to reach us. We harden our heart. He softens it with tenderness. We increase our sins. He intensifies His mercy. We complain. He becomes even more compassionate.

In response to the Hebrews' grumbling, God rained down bread from heaven for them. Each morning the dew covered the camp of the Hebrews. When the dew evaporated, fine flakes like hoarfrost covered the ground. Each day the people went out and gathered what they needed for that day (Ex 16:4). God gave the people a daily portion of manna in the desert to eat.

When the people first saw this, they had asked Moses, "What is this?" (in Hebrew: *man hu*). Hence the name "manna." Moses told them, "It is the bread the Lord has given us as food" (Ex 16:15). With the gift of manna, God provided the food they needed and, more than that, He renewed their hope. He not only nourished their body, but also He strengthened their spirit to continue the journey.

Teaching in the synagogue of Capernaum, Jesus proclaimed, "I am the bread of life. Your ancestors ate the manna in the wilderness, and yet they died. This is the bread that comes down from heaven, so that one may eat it and not die. I am the living bread that came down from heaven. Whoever eats this bread will live forever; and the bread that I will give is my flesh, for the life of the world" (Jn 6:48-51). Jesus is the Bread of Life. He is the New Manna come down from heaven.

God loved the people he freed from slavery. In their want, He fed them with bread from heaven to strengthen them on their journey to the Promised Land. God loves us so much that He has freed us from sin and death in our Baptism. As we make our way through this world to heaven, God feeds us with the very Body and Blood of Jesus. And at what cost!

In the time of Moses, the manna that came down from heaven was bruised in the mill to become bread to eat (Num 11:7-8). Jesus who came down from heaven and was brutally bruised, beaten, and crucified, now present in the Eucharist, is the New Manna. He is the living bread to feed us on our journey to the Promised Land. How much love Jesus has for us!

For the entire time of their wandering in the desert, God provided manna for the Hebrews. But once they entered the land of Canaan and ate of its produce, the manna stopped (Jos 5:12). As soon as the Hebrews could obtain a sufficient supply of bread in the ordinary way, God no longer provided them with manna miraculously. God does not squander His miracles. What we are capable of doing with the gifts He gives us in an ordinary way, He empowers us to do on our own.

During their journey through the wilderness, the manna had fallen six days a week, except on the Sabbath. In the wisdom of God, the very day it finally ceased was the day after the Sabbath, the first day of the week. That day would become the day of the Lord's Resurrection. Already God was indicating that the Risen Christ was to take the place of the manna. Unlike the manna of old given in a time of deprivation, Jesus in the Eucharist is given to us in times of plenty and in times of want. He comes to comfort us in our grief and to increase our joy. He is with us always to sustain us in our earthly pilgrimage.

Like the manna for the people of Israel, for every Christian generation the Eucharist is the indispensable nourishment that sustains them as they cross the desert of this world, parched by the ideological and economic systems that do not promote life but rather humiliate it. It is a world where the logic of power and possessions prevails rather than that of service and love; a world where the culture of violence and death is frequently triumphant.

Pope Benedict XVI, Homily,
Saint John Lateran, June 7, 2007

Prayer

O God, two things I ask of you;
do not deny them to me before I die;
Keep falsehood and lying far from me;
give me neither poverty nor riches,
but simply provide me with [my daily bread].
For if I have too much, I may deny you,
and say, "Who is the Lord?"
And if I am destitute, I may begin to steal
and profane the name of my God.

Prov 30:7-9

Additional prayers begin on page 161

CHAPTER 10

Our Daily Bread

"Give us this day our daily bread." Mt 6:11

Opening Prayer

O God, come to my assistance.
O Lord, make haste to help me.

Glory be to the Father
and to the Son
and to the Holy Spirit,
As it was in the beginning,
is now, and ever shall be,
world without end. Amen.

Act of Adoration

I place myself in the presence of Him, in whose Incarnate Presence I am before. I place myself there. I adore You, O my Savior, present here as God and as man, in soul and in body, in true flesh and blood. I acknowledge and confess that I kneel before that Sacred Humanity, which was conceived in Mary's womb, and lay in Mary's bosom; which grew up to twelve, wrought miracles, and spoke words of wisdom and peace; which in due season hung on the cross, lay in the tomb, rose from the dead, and now reigns in heaven.

I praise, and bless, and give myself wholly to Him, who is the true Bread of my soul, and my everlasting joy. *St. John Henry Newman*

Reflection

With a single miracle, God could have given the Hebrews all the bread they needed for their forty year journey to the Promised Land. But He did not. Instead, He commanded the Hebrews to gather the manna each day. On the day before the Sabbath, they were to gather a double portion so that they would not work on the Sabbath and yet have enough to eat.

God's gift of the manna was a double blessing. The portion of bread strengthened their body each day. It also strengthened their faith that God, who was providing in the present, would also provide in the future. The manna was their daily bread.

In teaching us the Our Father, Jesus told us to say, "Give us this day our daily bread" (Mt 6:11). When we say "this day" and "daily," we are not repeating ourselves. The New Testament Greek word rendered "daily" in English occurs only in this prayer and nowhere else in the Greek language. In translating the Bible into Latin, St. Jerome, like other Fathers of the Church, understood that Jesus was telling us to petition God not just for food for our table, but food for our soul. And so he translated the Greek word for "daily" with the Latin word *supersubstantialis*, that is, above the material or spiritual.

The Eucharist is our daily, spiritual food. It is Jesus, the Bread come down from heaven, who nourishes us each day. Already in the first days of the Church after Pentecost, believers "every day, united in the spirit, ... would assemble together in the temple. They would break bread in their homes..." (Acts 2:46). They understood their need for Jesus, their daily bread.

Each day we engage in a struggle for virtue in our own lives and for justice and peace in our world. We need the strength to resist temptations and to avoid sinning. Each day our faith is ridiculed; our morality, derided. We need the strength to speak out for the poorest, the weakest and the most vulnerable in our society. We need the courage to translate every day our beliefs into actions. For this reason, the Lord offers Himself to us as our daily bread.

When we receive Jesus as our daily bread, He strengthens our union with Him, He fills our souls with His Presence, and He makes us grow in all the virtues. Each time we receive the Eucharist, we are drawn into the heart of the Lord pierced open for all and we grow in our charity toward all people.

Because the Eucharist is our daily bread, the Church celebrates Mass every day. What a privilege to assist at Mass and to receive Jesus who comes to satisfy our deepest longings! In the Eucharist, all the other sacraments reach their goal, for we are joined to God in perfect union. As Pope St. John Paul once said, "For this reason it is good to cultivate in our hearts a constant desire for the sacrament of the Eucharist." This is the meaning of a spiritual communion.

When we are unable to go to Mass or when we are praying before the Blessed Sacrament, what a great devotion it is to make a spiritual communion! St. Teresa of Jesus wrote, "When you do not receive communion and you do not attend Mass, you can make a spiritual communion, which is a most beneficial practice." When we invite Jesus to come spiritually into our heart, we are expressing our hunger for Christ, our daily bread and our deep desire to be united with Him in living our faith.

St. Jean-Marie Vianney, the famous Curé of Ars, France, once said,

> If we are deprived of Sacramental Communion, let us replace it, as far as we can, by spiritual communion, which we can make every moment; for we ought to have always a burning desire to receive the good God. Communion

> is to the soul like blowing a fire that is beginning to go out, but that has still plenty of hot embers; we blow, and the fire burns again. After the reception of the Sacraments, when we feel ourselves slacken in the love of God, let us have recourse at once to spiritual communion. When we feel the love of God growing cold, let us instantly make a spiritual communion. When we cannot go to the church, let us turn towards the tabernacle; no wall can shut us out from the good God.

We can make a spiritual communion with words or even just with our heart's longing for Christ. Saint Leonard of Port Maurice once said, "If you practice the holy exercise of spiritual communion several times each day, within a month you will see your heart completely changed."

> *[Those who] cannot easily receive holy communion should do so at least by desire, so that with renewed faith, reverence, humility and complete trust in the goodness of the divine Redeemer, they may be united to Him in the spirit of the most ardent charity...For since by feasting upon the bread of angels we can ... become partakers of the sac-*

rifice..., continually experience within us the fruit of our redemption in a more efficacious manner.

Pope Pius XII, Mediator Dei, 117-118

Prayer

At Thy feet, O my Jesus, I prostrate myself and I offer Thee repentance of my contrite heart, which is humbled in its nothingness and in Thy holy presence. I adore Thee in the Sacrament of Thy love, the ineffable Eucharist. I desire to receive Thee into the poor dwelling that my heart offers Thee. While waiting for the happiness of sacramental communion, I wish to possess Thee in spirit. Come to me, O my Jesus, since I, for my part, am coming to Thee! May Thy love embrace my whole being in life and in death. I believe in Thee, I hope in Thee, I love Thee. Amen.

Servant of God Cardinal Rafael Merry del Val

May the heart of Jesus, in the Most Blessed Sacrament, be praised, adored, and loved with grateful affection, at every moment, in all the tabernacles of the world, even to the end of time. Amen.

Additional prayers begin on page 161

CHAPTER 11

The Dew and the Manna

"The manna would come down when the dew settled upon the camp at night."

Num 11:9

Opening Prayer

O God, come to my assistance.
O Lord, make haste to help me.

Glory be to the Father
and to the Son
and to the Holy Spirit,
As it was in the beginning,
is now, and ever shall be,
world without end. Amen.

Act of Adoration

I place myself in the presence of Him, in whose Incarnate Presence I am before. I place myself there. I adore You, O my Savior, present here as God and as man, in soul and in body, in true flesh and blood. I acknowledge and confess that I kneel before that Sacred Humanity, which was conceived in Mary's womb, and lay in Mary's bosom; which grew up to twelve, wrought miracles, and spoke

words of wisdom and peace; which in due season hung on the cross, lay in the tomb, rose from the dead, and now reigns in heaven. I praise, and bless, and give myself wholly to Him, who is the true Bread of my soul, and my everlasting joy. *St. John Henry Newman*

Reflection

Water enriches the earth as rain, sometimes as snow and sometimes ever so gently as dew. In the Holy Land, from the middle of June until the middle of September, rain, so necessary for farming, is scarce and the land is dry. By day, plants languish under the scorching sun. By night, the refreshing dew renews them. During these hot summer months, the dew that falls as a merciful gift from heaven is a welcome blessing, giving life and fruitfulness to the fields.

In Israel's forty year journey through the desert, God used dew to herald the gift of manna. The dew fell on the ground and, when it evaporated, there was the manna (Ex 16:14). The Second Eucharistic prayer harkens back to this event. At the consecration, the priest says, "Make holy, therefore, these gifts, we pray, by sending down your Spirit upon them like the dewfall, so that they may become for us the Body and Blood of our Lord Jesus Christ." This epiclesis, or invocation of the

Holy Spirit, envisions the Holy Spirit as the dew whose coming brings Christ, the bread of life, to us for our earthly pilgrimage to heaven.

The early Fathers of the Church recognized the role of the Holy Spirit in the gift of the Eucharist. In commenting on the dew that fell on Gideon's fleece, St. Irenaeus of Lyon, explained that the dew was the Holy Spirit who descended upon Jesus and who has been given to the Church (*Adversus Haereses* III, 17, 3). St. Cyril of Jerusalem reminds us that we "call upon God in his mercy to send his Holy Spirit upon the offerings before us, to transform the bread into the body of Christ and the wine into the blood of Christ. Whatever the Holy Spirit touches is sanctified and completely transformed" (*Catecheses*, XXIII, 7). Like the dew that falls upon the earth, the Holy Spirit comes down on the material elements of bread and wine, making them truly spiritual and life-giving as the Eucharist.

The gift of the Eucharist cannot be separated from the action and presence of the Holy Spirit. From the first moment of His conception in the womb of the Virgin Mary and throughout His life, the Holy Spirit was present working in and through Jesus. By the power of the Holy Spirit, Jesus was raised from the dead (Rom 8:11). And the Risen Lord gave the Holy Spirit as the first gift to the

Church. "It is through the working of the Spirit that Christ himself continues to be present and active in his Church, starting with her vital center which is the Eucharist" (Pope Benedict XVI, *Sacramentum Caritatis*, 12).

The Risen Jesus is now a "life-giving spirit" (1 Cor 15:45). As a result, when we receive Him in the Eucharist, He floods our souls with the gift of the Holy Spirit, enabling us to produce good works. And, when praying before the Eucharist, like the sun full blaze at noon, Jesus pours out the Holy Spirit on us, enkindling in us the fire of charity.

In Old Testament times, when Israel turned from God by worshiping the fertility gods of their pagan neighbors, Israel's love for God became as arid and lifeless as the parched desert. Israel was unfaithful. But God remained faithful. He told them through the prophet Hosea:

> I will forgive them for their apostasy,
> I will love them freely,
> for my wrath is turned away from them.
> I will be like the dew to Israel;
> they will blossom like a lily;
> They will strike root like the cedars of Lebanon.
>
> Hos 14:5-6

The Eucharist fulfills this prophecy.

In the Eucharist, God truly becomes the dew for us sinners. Receiving the Eucharist both sacramentally and spiritually makes our souls pure like the lily. It strengthens our will so that our thoughts, words, and actions, rooted in God's love, stand steadfast against any storm like the cedars of Lebanon. It makes us grow in holiness.

> *It is Christ who gives us…divine fullness through the action of the Holy Spirit. Thus, filled with divine life, Christians enter and live in the fullness of the whole Christ, which is the Church, and through the Church, in the new universe which is gradually being constructed… At the center of the Church is the Eucharist, where Christ is present and active in humanity and in the whole world by means of the Holy Spirit.*
>
> Pope St. John Paul II
> "Catechesis on the Holy Spirit"
> Castel Gondolfo, September 13, 1989

Prayer

O Lord Jesus Christ, Son of the living God, Who, by the will of the Father, with the cooperation of the Holy Spirit, have by Your death given life to the world, deliver me by this Your Most Sacred Body and Blood from all my sins and from every evil. Make me always cling to Your commandments, and never permit me to be separated from You. Who with the same God the Father and the Holy Spirit, live and reign, God, world without end. Amen.

Taken from the *Roman Missal*

May the heart of Jesus, in the Most Blessed Sacrament, be praised, adored, and loved with grateful affection, at every moment, in all the tabernacles of the world, even to the end of time. Amen.

Additional prayers begin on page 161

CHAPTER 12

The Showbread

"Set the bread of Presence on a table before me always." **Ex 25:30**

Opening Prayer

O God, come to my assistance.
O Lord, make haste to help me.

Glory be to the Father
and to the Son
and to the Holy Spirit,
As it was in the beginning,
is now, and ever shall be,
world without end. Amen.

Act of Adoration

I place myself in the presence of Him, in whose Incarnate Presence I am before. I place myself there. I adore You, O my Savior, present here as God and as man, in soul and in body, in true flesh and blood. I acknowledge and confess that I kneel before that Sacred Humanity, which was conceived in Mary's womb, and lay in Mary's bosom; which grew up to twelve, wrought miracles, and spoke words of wisdom and peace; which in due season hung on the cross, lay in the tomb,

rose from the dead, and now reigns in heaven. I praise, and bless, and give myself wholly to Him, who is the true Bread of my soul, and my everlasting joy. *St. John Henry Newman*

Reflection

Next to the ruins of the forum in Rome stands the Arch of Titus. This first century monument celebrates Rome's victory over the Jewish rebellion and the Fall of Jerusalem in 70 A.D. On an inner panel of the arch, there appears among the spoils of war an image of the table on which the showbread was placed in the Temple in Jerusalem. This was one of the most significant liturgical items of Jewish worship dating back to the time of the Exodus.

After Moses had ratified the covenant between God and the people, God summoned him to the top of Mt. Sinai. God then gave him detailed instructions on how to build the Tabernacle, also called the Tent of Meeting. Wherever Israel traveled in the desert, this portable tent went with them. It was the dwelling place of God among His people (Ex 25:8).

Commenting on God's commands concerning the Tabernacle, the 17th century Dutch theologian Hermann Witsius remarked, "God created the whole world in six days, but He used forty [days] to instruct Moses about the Tabernacle. Little over one chapter was needed to describe the structure of the world, but six [chapters] were used for the Tabernacle." Of particular note were God's commands about the showbread that was to be placed in the Tabernacle.

The showbread were twelve loaves of wheat bread. They represented the twelve tribes of Israel. These loaves were piled in two stacks of six on a golden table in front of the Holy of Holies. Each Sabbath, after the offering of the afternoon sacrifice at 3 P.M., the priests would replace the old loaves with new ones and then consume what was removed (Lev 24:5-9).

The showbread, made from the gifts of the land, symbolized the material blessings that God gave to His people. The showbread was continually replenished with fresh bread each Sabbath. Thus, they also bore the name "the loaves of permanent offering" (2 Chr 2:4). The showbread was a perpetual memorial of God's goodness to His people. For this reason, God commanded Moses, "Set the bread of the Presence on the table before me always" (Ex 25:30).

Besides signifying God's generosity to His people, the showbread also expressed Israel's gratitude to God. By placing before God the bread they had meticulously prepared, the people of Israel were acknowledging that God was providing for all their needs. He gave them what was essential for life. The loaves of bread, like our votive candles in church, were a visible sign of prayer raised to heaven thanking God for His gifts.

The showbread was called "the Bread of the Presence." The Hebrew *lechem hapānīm* (Bread of the Presence) literally means "Bread of the Face." It received its name from the fact that it was placed before the face of God and, in a real sense, revealed His face turned toward Israel with kindness and benevolence.

Maimonides, the great medieval Jewish philosopher, confessed that he had difficulty understanding the meaning of the showbread. He said, "I do not know the object of the table with the bread upon it continually, and up to this day I have not been able to assign any reason to this commandment." But now that Christ has given us the Eucharist, we can clearly understand how the Bread of Presence in the Old Testament prefigured this great gift and helps us gain a deeper appreciation of it.

The showbread was but a symbol of the gracious Presence of God with His people. The Eucharist is that Divine Presence. The showbread revealed to God's people the face of an all-loving God who stayed with them, protecting and guarding them. The Eucharist is Jesus who shows us the face of an all merciful God. As Jesus says to Philip at the Last

Supper, "Whoever has seen me has seen the Father" (Jn 14:9).

Jesus is "the image of the invisible God" (Col 1:15). From His coming among us at Bethlehem until His Ascension to the Father forty days after Easter, He showed us in a visible way the love and tenderness of God. Present in the Eucharist, He continues to show us the love of God who never abandons us on our earthly journey, protecting us against every evil. The Eucharist is the silent Presence of God in our midst.

The showbread stood before the Holy of Holies in the inner sanctuary, symbolizing the closeness of God and His people. However, a curtain separated the Holy of Holies from the showbread. When Christ died on the cross, that curtain in the Temple was torn in two and the way to God was opened. In the Eucharist, God draws near to us. The distance is bridged. For there is no greater closeness than God coming to dwell with us and in us through the Eucharist.

The showbread was renewed each Sabbath. It was a continual memorial. This reminded the people of the constant communion or fellowship which God desired to have with them. The Eucharist is the perpetual remembrance of Christ's sacrifice on the Cross. Christ Himself remains permanently in the Eucharist. In the

Eucharist, we find the perfect, uninterrupted fellowship of God with us. United to Christ in the Eucharist, we are drawn up into the very communion of the life of the Trinity.

On the three great feasts of Passover, Shavuot, and Sukkot, the Jews would make their pilgrimage to Jerusalem. According to the rabbis, when the pilgrims came to the Temple, the priests would hold up for them the golden table with the showbread. The priests would point to the bread and say, "Behold, God's love for you!" (Babylonian Talmud, *Menahoth* 29a).

When the Eucharist is placed in the monstrance, it is held up before us. And we are invited to look up at Jesus and know how truly beloved we are by God. It is not a mere sign. It is God truly with us. The Eucharist is truly the Bread of Presence. It is Jesus, our Lord and our God, waiting for us, eager to welcome our visit and offer us the intimacy of His love.

> *What happiness do we not feel in the presence of God, when we find ourselves alone at his feet, before the holy tabernacle! ... 'Come, my soul, redouble your ardor! You are here alone to adore your God! His look rests on you alone!' Ah! if we only had the angels' eyes! Seeing our Lord Jesus Christ here, on that altar, and looking at us, how we should love him! We should want*

to stay always at his feet; it would be a foretaste of heaven; everything else would become insipid to us.

St. John Vianney

Prayer

Most Merciful Jesus, whose very nature it is to have compassion on us and to forgive us, do not look upon our sins but upon our trust which we place in your infinite goodness. Receive us all into the abode of your Most Compassionate Heart, and never let us escape from it. We beg this of you by your love which unites you to the Father and the Holy Spirit. Amen.

May the heart of Jesus, in the Most Blessed Sacrament, be praised, adored, and loved with grateful affection, at every moment, in all the tabernacles of the world, even to the end of time. Amen.

Additional prayers begin on page 161

CHAPTER 13

The *todah* Sacrifice

"He who offers a sacrifice of thanksgiving honors me." **Psalm 50:23**

Opening Prayer

O God, come to my assistance.
O Lord, make haste to help me.

Glory be to the Father
and to the Son
and to the Holy Spirit,
As it was in the beginning,
is now, and ever shall be,
world without end. Amen.

Act of Adoration

I place myself in the presence of Him, in whose Incarnate Presence I am before. I place myself there. I adore You, O my Savior, present here as God and as man, in soul and in body, in true flesh and blood. I acknowledge and confess that I kneel before that Sacred Humanity, which was conceived in Mary's womb, and lay in Mary's bosom; which grew up to twelve, wrought miracles, and spoke words of wisdom and peace; which in due season hung on the cross, lay in the tomb,

rose from the dead, and now reigns in heaven. I praise, and bless, and give myself wholly to Him, who is the true Bread of my soul, and my everlasting joy. *St. John Henry Newman*

Reflection

The smoke of sacrifice rose unceasingly to heaven from the Temple in Jerusalem. For God had commanded that "the fire must always be kept burning. It must never go out" (Lev 6:13). The first seven chapters of Leviticus explain the five main categories of sacrifices to be offered to God on the fires of the altar. They were the Burnt Offerings, the Grain Offerings, the Communion Sacrifices, the Purification Offerings, and the Reparation Offerings. These sacrifices visibly expressed the desire of the individual and the community to restore and maintain an uninterrupted relationship with God.

Among the Communion Sacrifices, there was the important subcategory of *todah* (thanksgiving) sacrifice. This sacrifice was offered in gratitude for receiving a blessing or for being delivered from some life-threatening disease or danger. The offerer would bring a lamb to the Temple to be sacrificed. Along with the bloody sacrifice of the lamb, the priest would also offer up the unbloody offering of wine and bread (Lev 7:1-5, 11-15; 22:20-25; Num 15:7-10). In the case of Burnt Offerings, the sacrificed animal was wholly consumed in the fire. Of the offerings made for sin only the priests could eat. But priests and people ate of the Communion Sacrifices.

The law commanded the offerings of a Communion Sacrifice to be eaten on the very same day as the sacrifice. Nothing could be left over to the next day. According to the medieval French rabbi Rashi, one of the most influential Jewish commentators in history, this law, therefore, compelled the offerer to invite family and friends to feast on the lamb along with the bread and wine. Even if God had delivered the person quietly and unnoticed, thanking God did not remain a strictly personal act for a member of the community of faith. The blessing given to one person always affects others. By sharing in a communal meal, the participants expressed their fellowship with God and one another.

It was customary for a *todah* psalm to accompany the *todah* sacrifice. The psalm typically began as a lament and ended as praise. The lament portion recounted the suffering and circumstances afflicting the individual. It included a plea for deliverance. The second part of the psalm praised God for what He had done to deliver the person. Essential to a *todah* psalm was the narrative describing what the individual had suffered.

Psalm 22 follows the basic pattern of a *todah* psalm. The psalmist begins describing his intense suffering. He prays for God to save him from his enemies who seek his life. Then he praises God for delivering him. Finally, he concludes his prayer by inviting others to join him in a chorus of praise that spans generations.

Psalm 22 is a Messianic psalm. It holds a privileged place in the New Testament. It is the lens through which the early Christians understood the death of Jesus. In fact, the Passion narrative is a mosaic of references hewn from Psalm 22. Just a few examples will suffice.

As they pierced the hands and feet of the psalmist, so they crucified Jesus, also piercing His hands and feet with nails (Ps 22:17; Mt 27:35). As they divided the psalmist's garments and cast lots for his clothing, they did likewise with Jesus' garment (Ps 22:19; Mk 15:24). As they sneered and mocked the psalmist's trust in God, they mocked Jesus, taunting Him with the same insults (Psalm 22:8-9; Lk 23:35)). By weaving Psalm 22 within the very details of the Passion narrative, the early Christians were proclaiming that Christ's suffering and death were willed by God. He even foretold in this psalm the details of the Passion.

Jesus knew the Scriptures better than any other person. He himself understood His own death in light of Psalm 22. According to Matthew and Mark, Jesus spoke the first words of this psalm as His first words from the Cross. "About three o'clock in the afternoon, Jesus cried out in a loud voice, 'Eli, Eli, lema sabachthani?'—that is, 'My God. My God, why have you forsaken me?'" (Mt 27:46). Jesus knew the psalm by heart. In citing the first words of the psalm, He was praying the whole psalm in its entirety.

Even as He is undergoing the intense suffering of crucifixion and the painful agony of being rejected and abandoned, Jesus knows that the Father is with Him, delivering Him from death. When Jesus comes to the end of the psalm, with full confidence in the Father, He says:

> I will offer my praise to you in the great assembly...All the ends of the earth will remember and turn to the Lord. All the families of the nations will bow low before him...I will live for the Lord... Future generations will be told about the Lord so that they may proclaim to a people yet unborn the deliverance he has accomplished. *Ps 22:26-32*

On the Cross, Jesus offered Himself as the sacrifice for our sins. In praying this psalm, He widens our understanding of the great mystery of our redemption. This *todah* psalm joins Golgotha and the Upper Room as one great sacrifice. At the Last Supper, Jesus, the Lamb of God, institutes the Eucharist, already offering up His body and blood for our sins under the form of bread and wine. And He does so by offering thanks. The Eucharist is the perfect *todah* sacrifice.

In First Corinthians, Paul gives us the oldest New Testament account of the Institution of the Eucharist. His words clearly indicate that the early Christians were using a fixed tradition about celebrating the Last Supper.

> The Lord Jesus, on the night he was betrayed, took bread, and after giving thanks he broke it and said, "This is my body that is for you. Do this in remembrance of me." In the same fashion, after the supper, he also took the cup and said, "This cup is the new covenant in my blood. Whenever you drink it, do this in remembrance of me."
>
> *1 Cor 11:23-25*

Not only this account in Corinthians but all the other New Testament accounts of the Last Supper tell us that Jesus gave us the Eucharist *by giving thanks* (Mt 26:27; Mk 14:23; Lk 22:17 and 19). Jesus brings to fulfillment what the *todah* (thanksgiving) sacrifice of the Old Testament had foreshadowed.

At the Last Supper, Jesus not only makes present His own death in the bread broken and wine poured out, but also makes present His deliverance from death in the Resurrection. In giving us the Eucharist, Jesus thanks God and praises Him for rescuing Him from the tomb and raising Him up. And He invites His disciples to share the communion meal in which He Himself, the Lamb offered on the Cross, is now consumed under the sacramental signs of bread and wine that are now His Body and Blood.

No wonder, therefore, that what we do in remembrance of Him at Mass is called Eucharist. For "Eucharist" is the Greek word for "thanksgiving." In the second century, St. Justin Martyr wrote one of the earliest accounts of the Mass. Throughout his description, he uses over and over again the word "thanks."

> The apostles, in their recollections, which are called gospels, handed down to us what Jesus commanded them to do. They tell us that he took bread, gave *thanks* and said: Do this in memory of me. This is my body. In the same

> way he took the cup, he gave *thanks* and said: This is my blood... bread and wine and water are brought forward. The president offers prayers and gives *thanks*...those who are called by us deacons give to each of those present to partake of the bread and wine... over which the *thanksgiving* was pronounced.
>
> *St. Justin, First Apology 1, 65-67*

In the Eucharist, we give thanks for our deliverance from sin and eternal death. Our hearts overflow with gratitude for what Jesus has already accomplished for us. Filled with trust in God, we offer to God the homage of our lives and we join with other believers in singing God's glory. To celebrate the Eucharist is to truly honor God. As the psalmist says, "He who offers a sacrifice of thanksgiving honors me" (Ps 50:23). To live the Eucharist is to know the joy of being saved from eternal death. When we worship this great Sacrament, our life becomes each day a constant litany of thanks and praise.

In rabbinic literature, there is an ancient teaching that says, "In the coming Messianic age all sacrifices will cease, but the thanks offering [*todah*] will never cease" (*Pesquita*, 1). The Temple in Jerusalem is no more. The fire on its altar has gone out. Burnt offerings and sin offerings are no more. The Messiah has come. Jesus has fulfilled the promises of the Old Testament. In these last days, when all other sacrifices have ceased, the Eucharist, the perfect *todah* sacrifice, is daily offered on our altars.

> *Christ is present in the Eucharist, in the sacrament of His death and resurrection. In and through the Eucharist, you acknowledge the dwelling-place of the Living God in human history. For the Eucharist is the Sacrament of the Love which conquers death. It is the Sacrament of the Covenant, pure Gift of Love for the reconciliation of all humanity. It is the gift of the Real Presence of Jesus the Redeemer, in the bread which is His Body given up for us, in the wine which is His Blood poured out for all. Thanks to the Eucharist, constantly renewed among all peoples of the world, Christ continues to build His church: He brings us together in praise and thanksgiving for salvation, in the communion which only infinite love can forge.*
>
> Pope St. John Paul II
> "World Youth Day Homily"
> August, 1997, Paris, France

Prayer

I thank you, Eternal Father, for giving me as the food of my soul, the Body and Blood of your Only-begotten Son, our Lord Jesus Christ. May this Divine Food preserve and increase the union of my soul with you. May it purify me by repressing every evil inclination. Grant that it may be to me a pledge of a glorious resurrection on the last day. Through the same Christ our Lord. Amen.

May the heart of Jesus, in the Most Blessed Sacrament, be praised, adored, and loved with grateful affection, at every moment, in all the tabernacles of the world, even to the end of time. Amen.

Additional prayers begin on page 161

CHAPTER 14

Bethlehem

"And, you, Bethlehem . . . are by no means least..." **Mt 2:6**

Opening Prayer

O God, come to my assistance.
O Lord, make haste to help me.

Glory be to the Father
and to the Son
and to the Holy Spirit,
As it was in the beginning,
is now, and ever shall be,
world without end. Amen.

Act of Adoration

I place myself in the presence of Him, in whose Incarnate Presence I am before. I place myself there. I adore You, O my Savior, present here as God and as man, in soul and in body, in true flesh and blood. I acknowledge and confess that I kneel before that Sacred Humanity, which was conceived in Mary's womb, and lay in Mary's bosom; which grew up to twelve, wrought miracles, and spoke words of wisdom and peace; which in due

season hung on the cross, lay in the tomb, rose from the dead, and now reigns in heaven. I praise, and bless, and give myself wholly to Him, who is the true Bread of my soul, and my everlasting joy. *St. John Henry Newman*

Reflection

Giza built pyramids fit for a king. Athens gloried in the Acropolis and was envied by the wise. Rome boasted of her Colosseum and her military might. Jerusalem took pride in her Temple, the place of the worship of the true God. Yet, today not one of these receives as much praise in songs and hymns as the little town of Bethlehem.

Because of the census ordered by Caesar Augustus, Mary who was with child and Joseph traveled more than ninety miles from their residence in Nazareth to Joseph's hometown of Bethlehem. The ruler of the Roman Empire wanted to number his subjects so as to exact taxes from them. God willed to use him to bring to fulfillment His plan for the birth of the Messiah in the City of David.

At the time of Jesus' birth, Bethlehem was a small village just five miles south of Jerusalem. Its inhabitants numbered less than three hundred. Here Ruth had met Boaz and became the great grandmother of David. Here David was born and anointed king by Samuel.

However, by the first century, the glorious past of Bethlehem had dimmed.

Eight centuries before the coming of Christ, the prophet Micah had predicted that an honor greater than David's fame would crown this tiny hamlet. Moved by the Holy Spirit, Micah prophesied, "But from you, Bethlehem Ephrathah, among the tiniest clans of Judah, from you shall come forth...one who is to be ruler in Israel, one whose origins are from the distant past, from ancient times" (Mic 5:1). Not Jerusalem nor Rome nor Athens but Bethlehem God chose as the birthplace of His only-begotten Son.

In the hushed silence of the night, God wrapped the most astonishing event of human history in the garb of deepest humility. From the womb of the Virgin Mary, the lowly handmaid of the Lord, the Son of God entered our cold world, naked and dependent. Mary wrapped Him in swaddling clothes and placed Him gently in a manger. The Creator whom the world cannot contain was placed in the feedbox of dumb animals. He entrusted His life to Joseph, a humble laborer, to care for Him and protect Him. God became man and came among us with untold humility.

Not to potentates wielding their swords and not to priests engaged in sacred duties, not to the worldly rich, but to the earthly poor was

His coming announced. To the shepherds, the angel brought the announcement of Jesus' birth. They were keeping watch over their sheep near Migdal Eder. This was no ordinary place. Here were raised the lambs destined to be sacrificed in the Temple.

According to Jewish law, the lambs for sacrifice had to be born within five miles of Jerusalem and be without blemish. To keep those fragile lambs born fit for sacrifice, the shepherds would wrap them in swaddling clothes, protecting them from any bruise or break. Bethlehem was known for these sacrificial lambs. But with the angel's announcement, Bethlehem becomes renowned for the birth of the Lamb of God, the perfect victim who comes to lay down His life for all people.

Forty-five times the Old Testament names Jerusalem, the capital of King David's reign, as "the city of David." But, once Christ is born, Luke gives that title of honor to Bethlehem. Bethlehem, rising one hundred feet higher than Jerusalem, is thus exalted to a greater and more lasting dignity. It is the birthplace of the Son of God.

The fields surrounding Bethlehem produced an abundance of grain, figs, vines, almonds, and olives. Once, when there was a famine in the land of Moab during the time of the Judges, Naomi and her daughter-in-law Ruth returned to Bethlehem to find sustenance and support. Because of its rich fertility, the whole region was called "Ephrathah." This name means "fruitfulness" or "abundance." How fitting that this is the birthplace of Jesus. He comes to bring the abundance of grace to the world.

Located in the grain producing region of Old Testament times, "Bethlehem" literally means "House of Bread." How appropriate that Jesus is born here. During His public ministry after He multiplied the loaves and fish, Jesus identified Himself as the Bread of Life. And He explained to the crowds that He meant this literally. "I am the living bread that came down from heaven. Whoever eats this bread will live forever; and the bread that I will give is my flesh for the life of the world" (Jn 6:51). With these words, Jesus promised the Eucharist, His very Body and Blood as our food and drink.

Because of the Eucharist, Bethlehem is not an event lost in the faded light of the distant past. Its glory still shines bright upon us. Every Eucharist is Bethlehem for us. For, in every Eucharist, Jesus offers Himself to us as the Bread of Life. As the shepherds once said to each other on the night Jesus was born, we say to one another each time we go to Mass, "Come, let us go to Bethlehem to see this thing that has taken place, which the Lord has made known to us" (Lk 2:15). We go to welcome the Bread of Life into our lives.

In the Eucharist, He who humbled Himself to come among us as a man humbles Himself to be our food and drink. As St. Josemaria Escriva has said, in Bethlehem, in Nazareth, and on Calvary, we see the humility of Jesus. But the humility of Jesus in the Eucharist is even more astonishing. "More humiliation and more self-abasement still in the Sacred Host: more than in the stable, more than in Nazareth, more than on the Cross" (*The Way*, 533).

In Bethlehem, the Son of God hid His divinity in our humanity. Yet He could be seen and recognized as the son of Mary. On Calvary, the Son of Man hid His omnipotence in His suffering and death. "He had no beauty or majesty that would cause us to look at him...despised and shunned..." (Isa 53:2-3). But His total abasement on the Cross truly revealed Jesus and led a pagan centurion to exclaim, "Truly this man was the Son of God" (Mk 15:39).

However, in the Blessed Sacrament, neither His divinity nor His humanity is seen. He is hidden under the appearance of bread and wine. What humility! The child who cried in Mary's arms, the teacher who instructed the crowds, the compassionate healer at whose command demons fled and sickness was put to flight chooses to remain with us in the humble silence of the Eucharist. The Word wordless in the Eucharist with a love so ineffable it must be felt not spoken!

Thus, we come to the Eucharist with the humility of the shepherds to whom the angel brought the glad tidings of our Savior's birth. Before Jesus, we kneel in adoration like the shepherds, marveling at the wonder of God's love. The Lord comes to the weakest and the strongest among us. The repentant sinner and the struggling saint find in Him, "the true bread come down from heaven" (Jn 6:32). Before so great a sacrament, we humbly offer Him our soul to be His manger and our home His dwelling place.

> *O admirable height and stupendous condescension! O humble sublimity! O sublime humility! that the Lord of the universe, God and the Son of God, so humbles Himself that for our salvation He hides Himself under a morsel of bread. Consider, brothers, the humility of God and pour out your hearts before Him, and be humbled that you may be exalted by Him. Do not therefore keep back anything for yourselves that He may receive you entirely who gives Himself up entirely to you.*
>
> St. Francis of Assisi

Prayer

Lord Jesus, when you walked the earth,
Your humility obscured your Kingship.
Your meekness confused the arrogant,
Hindering them from grasping your purpose,
Your nobleness attending to the destitute.
Teach me to model after your eminence,
To subject my human nature to humility.
Grant me with a natural inclination
To never view myself greater than anyone.
Banish all lingering sparks of self-importance
That could elevate me greater than you.
Let my heart always imitate your humility.

Author Unknown

May the heart of Jesus, in the Most Blessed Sacrament, be praised, adored, and loved with grateful affection, at every moment, in all the tabernacles of the world, even to the end of time. Amen.

Additional prayers begin on page 161

CHAPTER 15

Emmanuel

"They shall name him 'Emmanuel,' a name that means 'God is with us.'" **Mt 1:23**

Opening Prayer

O God, come to my assistance.
O Lord, make haste to help me.

Glory be to the Father
and to the Son
and to the Holy Spirit,
As it was in the beginning,
is now, and ever shall be,
world without end. Amen.

Act of Adoration

I place myself in the presence of Him, in whose Incarnate Presence I am before. I place myself there. I adore You, O my Savior, present here as God and as man, in soul and in body, in true flesh and blood. I acknowledge and confess that I kneel before that Sacred Humanity, which was conceived in Mary's womb, and lay in Mary's bosom; which grew up to twelve, wrought miracles, and spoke words of wisdom and peace; which in due

season hung on the cross, lay in the tomb, rose from the dead, and now reigns in heaven. I praise, and bless, and give myself wholly to Him, who is the true Bread of my soul, and my everlasting joy. *St. John Henry Newman*

Reflection

From the time of King Herod until the destruction of Jerusalem, when Judea was under the Romans, one of the most popular names for Jewish men was Simon. The name means "one who hears" or "one who listens." How appropriate that the first person to hear Jesus' call to discipleship was the fisherman named Simon (Mk 1:16).

The day Simon became the first disciple to identify Jesus as the Messiah, Jesus coined the new name "Peter" for him. "Peter" means "rock;" and, Jesus so named him because Jesus was going to build His Church on the rock which was Peter (Mt 16:18). Throughout the Scriptures, names have meaning. For example, Adam means "man;" Benjamin, "son of my right hand;" David, "beloved;" and, Hannah (Ann) means "grace."

In the midst of a crisis in the 8th century before Christ, the prophet Isaiah coined a new name. Ahaz, the king of Judah, was being threatened by an alliance of the kings of Syria and Israel. Instead of trusting in God, Ahaz was planning to put his faith in Assyria to protect him from them. The prophet Isaiah boldly confronts the king. He promises that, despite the king's lack of trust in God, God would be faithful to the promise he made to David and protect the Davidic dynasty from being destroyed (2 Sam 7:5-16).

As a sign that this will happen, the prophet predicts that the threat of war will pass and, in gratitude, an unnamed woman will bear a son and name him "Emmanuel" (Isa 7:14).This is the first time this name appears in Scripture. It means "God with us." It expresses a truth repeated over and over again in the Scriptures: God is with His people to guide and protect them. From the moment God walks with Adam and Eve in the Garden of Eden (Gen 3:8) until God makes His final dwelling among His people (Rev 21:3), God never abandons His people.

The name "Emmanuel" appears twice in the Old Testament (Isa 7:14; 8:8). The name never appears again in the entire bible until Matthew gives this name to Jesus. When an angel informs Joseph to take Mary as his wife, he tells Joseph that the birth of her son will fulfill the meaning of the name "Emmanuel" that Isaiah first coined (Mt 1:23). In a way far beyond Isaiah's expectation, God was coming to be with us to protect and guide us in the person of Jesus.

The name "Emmanuel" reveals the deepest reality of Jesus. In Jesus, the infinite God took on our finite nature. The Creator became one with His creatures. The Eternal was born in time. The King became the servant of all. God who, from the first moment of creation, was for us became God with us forever.

The name "Emmanuel" sums up in a single word the mystery of the Incarnation and the Redemption. For Jesus, Emmanuel, came to be with us in joy and in sorrow, even to the point of taking on our sins on the Cross. "He was pierced for our offenses and crushed for our iniquity; the punishment that made us whole fell upon him, and by his bruises we have been healed" (Isa 53:5). Made one with us, He makes us one with God.

Matthew begins his gospel by telling us that Jesus is Emmanuel, "God with us." He ends his gospel with Jesus telling us that He will always be with us. The Risen Lord says, "Behold, I am with you always, to the end of the world" (Mt 28:20). Glorified and risen from the dead, Jesus continues to be Emmanuel.

With the gift of the Eucharist, the name "Emmanuel" becomes more than a consoling promise. It is the divine reality that we experience most intimately and personally. For "the Word [who] became flesh and dwelt among us" (Jn 1:14) now dwells among us in the Eucharist.

The Eucharist "is at one and the same time a Sacrifice-Sacrament, a Communion-Sacrament, and a Presence-Sacrament" (Pope St. John Paul II, *Redemptor Hominis*, IV, 20). As the Sacrament of Presence, the Eucharist is Christ, Body, Blood, Soul, and Divinity. It is Christ conceived in the womb of the Virgin Mary, Christ born in Bethlehem, Christ Crucified and Risen, Christ glorified and coming again.

Present in the Eucharist, the sacrament of divine love, Jesus is always drawing us to Himself. He makes Himself so near to us so that we can become closer to Him. Even after the celebration of Mass, Christ remains present in the Eucharist. "The Eucharist, in the Mass and outside of the Mass, is the Body and Blood of Jesus Christ, and is therefore deserving of the worship that is given to the living God, and to Him alone" (Pope St. John Paul II, Opening address in Ireland, Phoenix Park, September 29, 1979).

When we contemplate Jesus in the Eucharist, we stand before Him, as one stands before the sun, bathed in the transforming rays of His divine love. Looking at the Blessed Sacrament with love prolongs our communion and unites us more intimately with Jesus. Adoring Jesus in the Blessed Sacrament transforms our hearts and makes them more like His.

In the Eucharist, Jesus is "God with us" to pardon and forgive us. He is there to strengthen us with His grace and to sanctify us. He is there to draw us to Himself. What a consoling assurance: to look at the Blessed Sacrament and to know Jesus is with us in every joy and sorrow, in health and in sickness.

Jesus remains silent in the Eucharist. His silence is His loving invitation for us to speak to Him heart to heart. He is waiting for us to be present to Him who makes Himself truly present to us in the Blessed Sacrament. Adoring Jesus in the Eucharist gives us the joy "to draw water from the fountain of salvation" (Isa 12:3).

Adoration of the Eucharist is the logical consequence of the Real Presence. Before Christ, true God and true man, we humbly place ourselves. We acknowledge Him with the words of Thomas "My Lord and my God" (Jn 20:28). Adoration is an act of the most profound faith.

We offer our praise and gratitude to Christ for loving us and redeeming us by His death and resurrection. We also implore His mercy for our own sins and the sins of the world. As Pope St. John Paul II has said, "The Church and the world have a great need of Eucharistic worship. Jesus waits for us in this sacrament of love. Let us be generous with our time in going to meet Him in adoration and in contemplation..." (Pope St. John Paul II, *Dominicae Cenae*, 3)

In adoring the Blessed Sacrament, we unite ourselves with Christ. "For through him we... have access to the Father in the one Spirit" (Eph 2:18). Adoration deepens our union with the Father, Son, and Holy Spirit. It allows God to make us His dwelling place. Adoration is a foretaste of heaven.

> We become like that which we gaze upon. Looking into a sunset, the face takes on a golden glow. Looking at the Eucharistic Lord for an hour transforms the heart in a mysterious way as the face of Moses was transformed after his companionship with God on the mountain. Something happens to us similar to that which happened to the disciples at Emmaus. On Easter Sunday afternoon when the Lord met them, he asked why they were so gloomy. After spending some time in his presence, and hearing again the secret of spirituality—"The Son of Man must suffer to enter into his Glory"—their time with him ended and their "hearts were on fire."
>
> *Venerable Archbishop Fulton Sheen*

Prayer

My Lord Jesus Christ, who for the love which you bear us, remain night and day in this Sacrament full of compassion and love, awaiting, calling, and welcoming all who come to visit you, I believe that you are present in the Sacrament of the Altar. I adore you from the abyss of my nothingness, and I thank you for all the graces which you have bestowed upon me... My dear Savior, I unite all my affections with the affections of your most loving Heart, and I offer them, thus united, to your Eternal Father, and beseech him in your name to vouchsafe for your love, to accept and grant them. *St. Alphonse Liguori*

May the heart of Jesus, in the Most Blessed Sacrament, be praised, adored, and loved with grateful affection, at every moment, in all the tabernacles of the world, even to the end of time. Amen.

Additional prayers begin on page 161

CHAPTER 16

The Multiplication of the Loaves and Fish

"He looked up to heaven, blessed and broke the loaves and gave them to the disciples, and the disciples gave them to the crowds." Mt 14:19

Opening Prayer

O God, come to my assistance.
O Lord, make haste to help me.

Glory be to the Father
and to the Son
and to the Holy Spirit,
As it was in the beginning,
is now, and ever shall be,
world without end. Amen.

Act of Adoration

I place myself in the presence of Him, in whose Incarnate Presence I am before. I place myself there. I adore You, O my Savior, present here as God and as man, in soul and in body, in true flesh and blood. I acknowledge and confess that I kneel before that Sacred Humanity, which was conceived in Mary's womb, and lay in Mary's bosom; which grew up to twelve, wrought miracles, and spoke words of wisdom and peace; which in due season hung on the cross, lay in the tomb, rose from the dead, and now reigns in heaven. I praise, and bless, and give myself wholly to Him, who is the true Bread of my soul, and my everlasting joy. *St. John Henry Newman*

Reflection

All four evangelists tell us that Jesus multiplied bread and fish. In fact, the miracle of multiplying the five loaves and two fish to feed 5,000 men, in addition to the women and children, is the only miracle recorded in all four gospels (Mt 14:13-21; Mk 6:31-44; Lk 9:12-17; Jn 6:1-14). Matthew and Mark record a second miracle of feeding 4,000 with seven loaves and fish (Mt 15:32-39 and Mk 8:1-9). Without a doubt, the early Church regarded these miracles as the most significant event in the Galilean ministry of Jesus.

In all the accounts, the bread is more important than the fish. In three of the narratives, Jesus asks "How many loaves of bread do you have?" (Mk 6:38 and 8:5; Mt 15:34). And, at the end of the miracle, it is only the scraps of bread that are collected. All evangelists pen the significant action of Jesus with the same words they use to describe His giving us the Eucharist: *He took; He blessed; He gave thanks; He broke; He gave.* Thus, the evangelists record this miracle in a way to make us see that the multiplication of loaves not only foreshadows the Eucharist but also opens us to the meaning of this great mystery.

In the multiplication of loaves, Jesus satisfies the physical hunger of the crowds. In the Eucharist, He satisfies our deepest hunger for love and for God. Jesus feeds the 5,000 in an area not far from Capernaum in a Jewish setting. He feeds the 4,000 near the Decapolis in a Gentile setting. To Jews and Gentiles, Jesus is the Bread of Life. Jesus Himself can provide for the needs not only of the individual, but of the nations.

Before the feeding of the 5,000, Jesus had just crossed the Sea of Galilee to get away for a little rest. The rabble pursued Him. They would not leave Him alone. More miracles. More healings. More signs for themselves. But none of this matters to Jesus. They are hungry. They need to eat. The hour is inconvenient. The demand unreasonable. Yet Jesus responds as the one who serves. The Eucharist is the sacrament of service to others. It fills us with love that looks beyond our comfort and our own interests and impels us to meet the needs of others.

In John's account of the miracle, Jesus sees the crowds coming to Him and He anticipates the need to feed them. Love opens our eyes to others' hunger. Eucharistic love is always spontaneous. It does not wait to act. Need noticed, action taken.

Before feeding the crowds, Jesus turns to Philip. Whenever we meet Philip with Jesus, it is always Philip doing the questioning. But, Jesus gently reverses the role and questions him, "Where are we to buy bread for them to eat?" (Jn 6:5). Philip informs Jesus that "Two hundred days' wages would not buy enough bread for each of them to have a small piece" (Jn 6:7). And, Andrew points to a young boy with five barley loaves and two fish. And, then he adds, "What help would that be among so many?"(Jn 6:9).

Jesus takes the small amount of food available, insufficient by human standards, and feeds the thousands with more than they could eat. The apostles see with their own eyes His infinite power. They also witness His compassion and concern for others.

At the heart of the Eucharist is Jesus' compassion for those in need. When we come to the Eucharist, we come to Jesus whose feet are bleeding and tired from walking miles in search of work and a decent living. We come to Jesus whose hands are calloused from hard labor and whose eyes are wet with the tears of the addict, the alcoholic and the bereaved.

By contemplating the Eucharist, we are led to follow Jesus' example of compassionate outreach to others. For "the Eucharist draws us into Jesus' act of self-oblation. More than just statically receiving the incarnate Logos, we enter into the very dynamic of His self-giving" (Pope Benedict XVI, *Deus Caritas Est*, 13). The Eucharist moves us to self-giving actions towards the members of our human family who face injustice in any way.

A passionate devotion to Jesus in the Eucharist always means a compassionate heart and a helping hand for those in need. As St. John Chrysostom once said, "Do you wish to honor the body of Christ? Do not ignore him when he is naked... What good is it if the Eucharistic table is overloaded with golden chalices when your brother is dying of hunger. Start by satisfying his hunger and then with what is left you may adorn the altar as well." Truly honoring the mystery of Eucharist always entails alleviating the miseries of our brothers and sisters.

> Union with Christ is also union with all those to whom he gives himself. I cannot possess Christ just for myself; I can belong to him only in union with all those who have become, or who will

become, his own. Communion draws me out of myself towards him, and thus also towards unity with all Christians. We become "one body," completely joined in a single existence. Love of God and love of neighbor are now truly united: God incarnate draws us all to himself. We can thus understand how agape also became a term for the Eucharist: there God's own agape comes to us bodily, in order to continue his work in us and through us... "Worship" itself, Eucharistic communion, includes the reality both of being loved and of loving others in turn.

Pope Benedict XVI
Deus Caritas Est, 14

Prayer

O God, in the Eucharist, you have given us your Son Jesus whose heart is full of compassion for all your children. Strengthen us by the reception and worship of the Blessed Sacrament so that we may truly become your family where all are welcome at the banquet of life. May our eyes be open to those in need. May we be eager always to heal the divisions that separate us. And, may our words and deeds bring your justice and peace to all. Amen.

May the heart of Jesus, in the Most Blessed Sacrament, be praised, adored, and loved with grateful affection, at every moment, in all the tabernacles of the world, even to the end of time. Amen.

Additional prayers begin on page 161

CHAPTER 17

Eucharistic Discourse in Capernaum

"For my flesh is true food, and my blood is true drink." **Jn 6:55**

Opening Prayer

O God, come to my assistance.
O Lord, make haste to help me.
Glory be to the Father
and to the Son
and to the Holy Spirit,
As it was in the beginning,
is now, and ever shall be,
world without end. Amen.

Act of Adoration

I place myself in the presence of Him, in whose Incarnate Presence I am before. I place myself there. I adore You, O my Savior, present here as God and as man, in soul and in body, in true flesh and blood. I acknowledge and confess that I kneel before that Sacred Humanity, which was conceived in Mary's womb, and lay in Mary's bosom; which grew up to twelve, wrought miracles, and spoke

words of wisdom and peace; which in due season hung on the cross, lay in the tomb, rose from the dead, and now reigns in heaven. I praise, and bless, and give myself wholly to Him, who is the true Bread of my soul, and my everlasting joy. *St. John Henry Newman*

Reflection

Jesus chose the seaside town of Capernaum to be the center of His ministry in Galilee. There He preached to the amazement of the crowds. His words and His miracles attracted many. But, the day Jesus gave His famous discourse on the Eucharist in the synagogue of Capernaum, He stunned His listeners and left them perplexed and wondering what He meant (Jn 6:22-59).

The day before this discourse, Jesus had fed the 5,000 with the miracle of the loaves and fish. The barley harvest had not yet occurred. And so, at this time, right before the Passover, the price of bread was higher. Jesus' miracle stirred the great interest of the multitude. They sought Him out for more bread. They had witnessed the miracle, but had not understood it as a sign of a greater gift yet to come.

The crowd tells Jesus that Moses gave their ancestors "bread from heaven" (Jn 6:31). In response, Jesus proclaims, "I am the bread of life; whoever comes to me will never be hungry, and whoever believes in me will never be thirsty" (Jn 6:35). When the Jews murmur and question what He means, He makes it clear that He is not speaking metaphorically. He says,

> Amen, amen, I say to you, unless you eat the flesh of the Son of Man and drink his blood, you do not have life within you. Whoever feeds upon my flesh and drinks my blood has eternal life, and I will raise him on the last day. For my flesh is real food, and my blood is real drink.
> Jn 6:53-55

Four times in His discourse on the Eucharist in Capernaum, Jesus refers to Himself as the Bread of life (Jn 6:35, 41, 48, 51). And five times Jesus explains that He is the bread of life inasmuch as we eat His very Body and Blood (Jn 6: 51, 53, 55, 56, 57). In fact, in the Greek text of Jesus' discourse, the verb φάγω (phago) is used nine times (Jn 6:31 twice, 49, 50, 51 twice, 52, 53, 58). That word literally means "to consume physically" And the word τρώγω (trogo), a more literal word meaning "to chew," or "to feed upon," is used four times (Jn 6:54, 56, 57, 58). This shocks His listeners. How is it possible to eat the flesh and blood of Jesus?

When speaking to Nicodemus, Jesus corrects Nicodemus' misunderstanding of Jesus' words about being born again. Nicodemus took those words literally. Jesus tells him that He is speaking metaphorically. When the crowd cannot accept the literal meaning of eating Jesus' Body and Blood, Jesus does not correct them.

Some of those who came to Capernaum and heard Jesus speak of the Eucharist walked away in disbelief. Some of those who had been following Him as disciples parted company with Him. And, even among the Twelve Apostles, Judas separates himself from the others at this point. His betrayal in the Garden of Gethsemane begins with his rejection of Jesus' gift of the Eucharist. For it is only in accepting the Eucharist and receiving this great gift with faith that we avoid betraying Jesus with our sins.

Jesus promises the Eucharist just one year before His death on the Cross. What great love the Savior has for us that He already is planning to give Himself to us as our food and drink for eternal life! We may say: "I should like to see His face, His garments, His shoes. You do see Him, you touch Him, you eat Him. He gives Himself to you, not only that you may see Him, but also to be your food and nourishment (St. John Chrysostom).

He is The Bread sown in the virgin, leavened in the Flesh, molded in His Passion, baked in the furnace of the

Sepulcher, placed in the Churches, and set upon the Altars, which daily supplies Heavenly Food to the faithful.

St. Peter Chrysologus

Prayer

You come to me and unite yourself intimately to me
under the form of nourishment.
Your Blood now runs in mine,
Your Soul, Incarnate God, compenetrates mine,
giving courage and support.
What miracles! Who would have ever imagined such!

St. Maximilian Kolbe

May the heart of Jesus, in the Most Blessed Sacrament, be praised, adored, and loved with grateful affection, at every moment, in all the tabernacles of the world, even to the end of time. Amen.

Additional prayers begin on page 161

CHAPTER 18

The Institution of the Eucharist

"This is my body...This is
my blood..." Mk 14:22-24

Opening Prayer

O God, come to my assistance.
O Lord, make haste to help me.

Glory be to the Father
and to the Son
and to the Holy Spirit,
As it was in the beginning,
is now, and ever shall be,
world without end. Amen.

Act of Adoration

I place myself in the presence of Him, in whose Incarnate Presence I am before. I place myself there. I adore You, O my Savior, present here as God and as man, in soul and in body, in true flesh and blood. I acknowledge and confess that I kneel before that Sacred Humanity, which was conceived in Mary's womb, and lay in Mary's bosom; which grew up to twelve, wrought miracles, and spoke

words of wisdom and peace; which in due season hung on the cross, lay in the tomb, rose from the dead, and now reigns in heaven. I praise, and bless, and give myself wholly to Him, who is the true Bread of my soul, and my everlasting joy. *St. John Henry Newman*

Reflection

When Jesus began His Passion, He went forth from the Upper Room to suffer and die on the Cross. But His disciples went forth to deny, betray, and abandon Him. Even so, His heart, burdened for our sins, was so full of love that He would not abandon us. In the dimly lit room of the Last Supper, Jesus instituted the Eucharist so that, in sharing His Body given for us and His Blood outpoured for us, we could always be one with Him and pass from darkness into light, from death to life.

The New Testament gives us four accounts of the institution of the Eucharist (Mt 26:26-30; Mk 14:22-24; Lk 22:14-20 and 1 Cor 11: 23-26). Matthew and Mark are very close in the way they recount the event. They reflect the liturgical tradition of celebrating the Eucharist which originated with Aramaic-speaking Christians. Luke and Paul, on the other hand, are very close to each other and reflect the Eucharist as celebrated among Greek-speaking Christians.

Paul gives us the earliest account of the institution of the Eucharist. In 1 Cor 11:23-25, he says,

> For what I received from the Lord I handed on to you: the Lord Jesus on the night he was betrayed, took bread, and after giving thanks he broke it and said, "This is my body that is for you, do this in remembrance of me." In the same fashion, after the supper, he also took the cup and said, "This cup is the new covenant in my blood. Whenever you drink it, do this in remembrance of me."

Paul introduces his account of the institution of the Eucharist with the well-known formula *What I received...I handed on to you.* The rabbis would use this expression when handing on to their disciples a tradition that did not originate with them, but from someone of greater authority. Thus, Paul is emphasizing the fact that the Eucharist comes directly from Jesus Himself. Whether Paul received this tradition from the Lord in a vision or from the Church at Antioch matters little. For Paul, Jesus gave the Eucharist to the Church as a gift of inestimable value.

Keep in mind that Paul is writing to the Corinthians about twenty years after the death of Jesus and certainly before either Matthew, Mark, or Luke has penned his inspired gospel. This tradition, passed on in fixed formula by Paul, means that, from the very beginning, the disciples of Jesus were celebrating the Eucharist in fidelity to Jesus' own mandate "Do this in memory of me" (Lk 22:19; 1 Cor 11:24-25).

Luke, who wrote his gospel and Acts of the Apostles, was a companion of Paul. He lists as one of the distinguishing characteristics of the first Christians their coming together to celebrate the Eucharist. "They devoted themselves to the teaching of the apostles and to the communal fellowship, to the breaking of the bread and to prayers" (Acts 2:42; also Acts 2:46; 20:7). The Eucharist was then and is today the very source of the Church's growth.

When Jesus breaks the bread and says, "This is my body which will be *given* for you" (Lk 22:19), He is speaking of His death on the Cross. For it was on the Cross that Jesus "*gave* himself for our sins to deliver us" (Gal 1:4). When He speaks about His blood "which will be shed (literally, ἐκχυννόμενον: being poured out) on behalf of many for the forgiveness of sins" (Mt 26:28, also Mk 14:24; Lk 22:20), He likewise is referring to His death.

In instituting the Eucharist, Christ "did not merely say: 'This is my body,' 'this is my blood,' but went on to add: 'which is given for you,' 'which is poured out for you' (Lk 22:19-20). Jesus did not simply state that what He was giving them to eat and drink was His body and His blood; Jesus also expressed *its sacrificial meaning* and made sacramentally present His sacrifice which would soon be offered on the Cross for the salvation of all" (Pope St. John Paul II, *Ecclesia de Eucharistia*, 12). "The sacrifice of Christ and the sacrifice of the Eucharist are one single sacrifice" (*Catechism of the Catholic Church*, 1367).

Thus, at every Eucharist, we are with Christ at the Last Supper as He anticipates and already makes present to His disciples the redemptive mystery of His death. We are at the foot of the Cross with Mary and John as Jesus offers His life for our salvation. So great is Christ's love for us that He not only saved us by His Passion, Death, and Resurrection, but He gave us in the Eucharist a way to be with Him as He accomplishes our redemption. And so "we must sacrifice ourselves to God, each day and in everything we do, accepting all that happens to us for the sake of the Word, imitating his passion by our sufferings, and honoring his blood by shedding our own. We must be ready to be crucified" (St. Gregory Nazianzen, *Oratio* 45, 23).

Recognize in this bread what hung on the cross, and in this chalice what flowed from His side...whatever was in many and varied ways announced beforehand in the sacrifices of the Old Testament pertains to this one sacrifice which is revealed in the New Testament.

St. Augustine, Sermon 3, 2

Prayer

Lord Jesus Christ, eternal King, God and man,
crucified for mankind,
look upon me with mercy and hear my prayer,
for I trust in you.
Have mercy on me,
full of sorrow and sin,
for the depth of your compassion never ends.
Praise to you, saving sacrifice,
offered on the wood of the cross for me
and for all mankind.
Praise to the noble and precious blood,
flowing from the wounds of my crucified
Lord Jesus Christ
and washing away the sins of the whole world.

Remember, Lord, your creature,
whom you have redeemed with your blood.
I repent of my sins,
and I long to put right what I have done.
Merciful Father, take away
all my offenses and sins;
purify me in body and soul,
and make me worthy to taste the holy of holies.

St. Ambrose

May the heart of Jesus, in the Most Blessed Sacrament, be praised, adored, and loved with grateful affection, at every moment, in all the tabernacles of the world, even to the end of time. Amen.

Additional prayers begin on page 161

CHAPTER 19

A Remembrance

"Do this in remembrance of me."
1 Cor 11:24-25

Opening Prayer

O God, come to my assistance.
O Lord, make haste to help me.

Glory be to the Father
and to the Son
and to the Holy Spirit,
As it was in the beginning,
is now, and ever shall be,
world without end. Amen.

Act of Adoration

I place myself in the presence of Him, in whose Incarnate Presence I am before. I place myself there. I adore You, O my Savior, present here as God and as man, in soul and in body, in true flesh and blood. I acknowledge and confess that I kneel before that Sacred Humanity, which was conceived in Mary's womb, and lay in Mary's bosom; which grew up to twelve, wrought miracles, and spoke words of wisdom and peace; which in due season hung on the cross, lay in the tomb,

rose from the dead, and now reigns in heaven. I praise, and bless, and give myself wholly to Him, who is the true Bread of my soul, and my everlasting joy. *St. John Henry Newman*

Reflection

The ancient Hebrew had no word for history. We record events and confine them to the past. We chronicle history. Not so the people of the Bible. For them, they remembered events. And it was never merely the recollection of something that had occurred in the distant past. When they remembered the Sabbath, they actually entered into God's eternal rest.

In the Hebrew mentality, all events are objectively present in God's eternal memory. And so when God remembers an event of the past, it is actually eternally present in God. And, when the Chosen People remember the foundational events of their faith, those events are present to those events. An example will help to understand.

In giving instructions for the Passover, God says to Moses, "This day shall be a memorial (*zikkaron*/anamnesis) for you. You shall celebrate it as a feast of the Lord, from generation to generation..." (Ex 12:14). Today, in the celebration of the Passover, our Jewish brothers and sisters recite all the prayers and readings of the Seder in the present tense. It is not something that just happened in the past to their ancestors. It is something happening to them as they remember it. For, as the rabbis of the Mishnah clearly taught, "in every generation a man must so regard himself as if he himself came out of Egypt, for it is written, 'And thou shalt tell thy son in that day saying, it is because of that which the Lord did for me when I came forth out of Egypt'" (Mishnah *Pesachim*, 10:5).

Thus, in the biblical way of thinking, remembrance (*zikkaron*/anamnesis) is not simply recollecting the past in which the distance between the event and the present is maintained. Rather, remembrance makes the events of sacred history present to the community of faith and allows believers to participate in them.

It is within the context of this Jewish understanding of remembrance that, at the Last Supper, Jesus commanded us to celebrate the Eucharist, saying, "Do this in remembrance of me" (1 Cor 11:24 and 25). With His sovereign authority as God, Jesus is taking the command God gave Moses to do a remembrance (*zikkaron*/ anamnesis)) of the Exodus in the Passover celebration and infusing it with a richer and deeper meaning. The Church is now to celebrate the Eucharist as a memorial or remembrance of the Paschal Mystery. In this way, His followers in every generation can share in His death and resurrection, His exodus from this world to the Promised Land.

The disciples hearing Jesus speak of the Eucharist as a remembrance or memorial were very familiar with the worship in the Temple in Jerusalem. Every Sabbath when the twelves loaves of showbread placed in the sanctuary were exchanged for fresh ones, the incense that had been placed near them in golden bowls was thrown on the fire of the altar as “a memorial offering” (Lev 24:7). The incense took the place of the showbread that had represented the people of God. And so, in the incense burned on the fire, it was all the people of God that was being offered up as a bloodless sacrifice to God.

Likewise, the Eucharist is a memorial offering that makes present in an unbloody way the bloody sacrifice of the Cross. And it includes the whole Church. As St. Augustine taught, [the Eucharist] “is the sacrifice of Christians: that we...are one body in Christ. The Church celebrates this mystery in the sacrament of the altar, as the faithful know, and there she shows them clearly that in what is offered, she herself is offered” (St. Augustine, *De Civitate Dei*, X, 6).

Thus, all of us who are the Church are offered up with Christ in the Eucharist. This offering radically transforms our entire life. For all we do and say in union with Christ Crucified now becomes, like the incense thrown on the fire, a fragrance pleasing to God.

Thus, in every Eucharist, we do not merely keep alive in our minds that memory of Christ's death and resurrection. But we ourselves become true sharers in His dying and rising. As we offer ourselves in union with Him, every aspect of our lives becomes Eucharistic. We are transformed and, in a world that would enslave us to sin, we come to enjoy the true freedom of the children of God.

> *The Eucharist...embraces the concrete, everyday existence of the believer... There is nothing authentically human—our thoughts and affections, our words and deeds—that does not find in the sacrament of the Eucharist the form it needs to be lived to the full. Here we can see the full human import of the radical newness brought by Christ in the Eucharist: the worship of God in our lives cannot be relegated to something private and individual, but tends by its nature to permeate every aspect of our existence. Worship pleasing to God thus becomes a new way of living our whole life, each particular moment of*

which is lifted up, since it is lived as part of a relationship with Christ and as an offering to God.

Pope Benedict XVI,
Sacramentum Caritatis, 71

Prayer

O Jesus, through the Immaculate Heart of Mary, I offer you my prayers, works, joys, and sufferings of this day in union with the Holy Sacrifice of the Mass throughout the world. I offer them for all the intentions of Your Sacred Heart: the salvation of souls, reparation for sin, and the reunion of all Christians. Amen.

May the heart of Jesus, in the Most Blessed Sacrament, be praised, adored, and loved with grateful affection, at every moment, in all the tabernacles of the world, even to the end of time. Amen.

Additional prayers begin on page 161

CHAPTER 20

Table Fellowship with God

"Whenever you eat this bread and drink this cup, you proclaim the death of the Lord until he comes." **1 Cor 11:26**

Opening Prayer

O God, come to my assistance.
O Lord, make haste to help me.

Glory be to the Father
and to the Son
and to the Holy Spirit,
As it was in the beginning,
is now, and ever shall be,
world without end. Amen.

Act of Adoration

I place myself in the presence of Him, in whose Incarnate Presence I am before. I place myself there. I adore You, O my Savior, present here as God and as man, in soul and in body, in true flesh and blood. I acknowledge and confess that I kneel before that Sacred Humanity, which was conceived in Mary's womb, and lay in Mary's bosom; which grew up to twelve, wrought miracles, and spoke

words of wisdom and peace; which in due season hung on the cross, lay in the tomb, rose from the dead, and now reigns in heaven. I praise, and bless, and give myself wholly to Him, who is the true Bread of my soul, and my everlasting joy. *St. John Henry Newman*

Reflection

The early Christian basilicas in Rome, the Cathedrals of the Middle Ages, the Gothic Revival churches in 20th century America and the more contemporary constructions of recent years all share the same purpose. The church building is meant to be "a sacred building destined for divine worship… More than just a place where we gather, the church building makes visible the Church living in this place, the dwelling of God with us reconciled and united in Christ" (*Catechism of the Catholic Church*, 1180).

Central to every Catholic church, therefore, is the altar on which the Eucharist is celebrated. For the Eucharist is the summit and source of the Church's life. The Eucharist makes the Church. And the Church makes the Eucharist. No Eucharist, no Church. The Eucharist is the Church's most sacred treasure, because the Eucharist is the Lord Jesus.

So great is the mystery of the Eucharist that it cannot be straight-jacketed into a single concept or explanation. Jesus gifted the Church with the Eucharist at the Last Supper. On the evening before He died, He celebrated God's deliverance of Israel and the redemption He Himself was accomplishing for all. He did this in the context of the Passover meal.

The very giving of the Eucharist reminds us of the structure of a meal. "Take, eat... Then he took a cup and... gave it to them, saying: Drink from it, all of you" (Mt 26:26-27). The Eucharist is the meal in which we enjoy table fellowship with the Lord. When we worthily receive the Eucharist, we enter into a profound communion with Jesus. He abides in us and we in Him (Jn 15:4).

Israel celebrated communion sacrifices in which part of the victim was offered to God and another portion given to the faithful to eat. Thus Israel expressed her desire to be one with God. When God ratified the covenant with Israel, Moses, Aaron and his two sons Nadab and Abihu, along with the seventy elders, went up the mountain. In a very rare sentence in the entire Old Testament, we are told, "they saw God and yet continued to eat and drink" (Ex 24:11).

At the very birth of God's chosen people, the meal on the mountain prefigured the fellowship which God wishes to establish with all His children. Today, as we sit down at the

Lord's Table, we eat and drink in His sight. We share in the very life of God Himself.

All the narratives of the Last Supper (Mt 26:26-28: Mk 14:22-24: Lk 22:19-20; and 1 Cor 11:23-25) help us understand the Eucharist as not just a meal but as sacrifice. Jesus gives His body broken for us and His blood poured out for us. Jesus is the Suffering Servant who is offering Himself in sacrifice, pouring out His blood as the new covenant. He offers Himself in place of humanity and for the salvation of all (Isa 42:1-9; 49:8). The Eucharist is a sacrifice, not repeated again and again, but the one sacrifice of the Cross made present to us in every age.

At the same time that the Eucharist makes present what occurred in the past, it also impels us towards the future. The Liturgy itself reminds us of this in the acclamation following the consecration: "When we eat this bread and drink this cup, we proclaim your death, O Lord, until you come again." The Eucharist is an eschatological event.

Christ who will come again at the end of time comes to us in every Eucharist. This eschatological aspect makes the Eucharist an event that draws us up into heaven. Thus, the Eucharist fills our life journey with hope. In every Eucharist, we enter the Holy of Holies and we are sanctified (see Heb 9:11-14). The

Eucharist is the privileged place where life becomes sacred. The Eucharist makes our life a sacred adventure of ever-deepening communion with God.

> *When you see the Lord sacrificed, laid upon the altar, and the priest standing and praying over the victim, and all the worshippers empurpled with that precious blood, can you then think that you are still among men, and standing upon the earth? Are you not, on the contrary, straightway translated to heaven, and casting out every carnal thought from the soul, do you not, with disembodied spirit and pure reason, contemplate the things which are in heaven?*
>
> St. John Chrysostom,
> *De Sacerdotio*, III, 4

Prayer

Lord Jesus, we praise and thank you for giving us the Eucharist as even now a foretaste of the banquet of heaven. As we honor and worship your Body and Blood, graciously strengthen our faith, give us rest from our labors, comfort in our sorrows, turn our gaze toward the eternal wedding feast for which we long and, even now, give us the joy of being one with you who live and reign forever and ever. Amen.

May the heart of Jesus, in the Most Blessed Sacrament, be praised, adored, and loved with grateful affection, at every moment, in all the tabernacles of the world, even to the end of time. Amen.

Additional prayers begin on page 161

CHAPTER 21

On the Road to Emmaus

"Stay with us, for it is nearly evening..."
Lk 24:29

Opening Prayer

O God, come to my assistance.
O Lord, make haste to help me.

Glory be to the Father
and to the Son
and to the Holy Spirit,
As it was in the beginning,
is now, and ever shall be,
world without end. Amen.

Act of Adoration

I place myself in the presence of Him, in whose Incarnate Presence I am before. I place myself there. I adore You, O my Savior, present here as God and as man, in soul and in body, in true flesh and blood. I acknowledge and confess that I kneel before that Sacred Humanity, which was conceived in Mary's womb, and lay in Mary's bosom; which grew up to twelve, wrought miracles, and spoke words of wisdom and peace; which in due

season hung on the cross, lay in the tomb, rose from the dead, and now reigns in heaven. I praise, and bless, and give myself wholly to Him, who is the true Bread of my soul, and my everlasting joy. *St. John Henry Newman*

Reflection

Of all the stories Luke ever told of the Risen Lord, the most memorable is the Emmaus account. Cleopas and another unnamed disciple have left Jerusalem. St. Cyril of Alexandria says that both men were part of the seventy disciples Jesus sent out on mission. And the second disciple was a man named Simon. Close to Jesus in His life, they are now distant from Him in His death. Sad. Downcast. Christ had been crucified. He is dead. Their hopes now entombed with Him.

But it is Easter Sunday. And in Jerusalem, the tomb is empty. As they travel away from the events that took place in the Holy City, the Risen Lord draws near to them. He joins their journey to Emmaus. As they walk, they talk. But there is something very unusual here. Every other time the Risen Lord appears, He speaks a word and He is recognized. But not here!

At the tomb Easter morning, Mary Magdalene weeps. Jesus speaks one word: "Mary." And she falls down in adoration. In the Upper

Room where Jesus had celebrated the Last Supper, He appears a second time. To doubting Thomas, who had been absent when He appeared on Easter Sunday night, He now says, "Put your fingers into my wounds." And Thomas immediately confesses, "My Lord and my God." The most profound confession of faith found on the lips of the apostles in any of the gospels!

But on the road to Emmaus, the two disciples walk and talk to Jesus. He explains all the Scriptures that foretell His death. Their hearts burn within. Yet they do not recognize Him. He is present, yet somehow hidden. The Risen Lord is patient with their slow understanding, their halting faith. Jesus does not hurry or hasten the moment for them to embrace His Presence. Emmaus is the Resurrection Appearance of Divine Patience and the Eucharist is the Sacrament of Divine Patience.

In the Eucharist, Jesus is with us. He is the Risen Lord before us. All the while, He speaks to us. In the depths of our hearts quieted from the cares of the world, Jesus makes His presence known. In our mind searching for truth, He speaks the truth of His abiding love beyond words. Love never compels. Love never coerces a response. This great sacrament is Jesus loving us, waiting for us. It is Jesus longing to invite us to remain with Him like the two disciples on the road to Emmaus.

When Cleopas and the other disciple sense that Jesus is about to leave them, they earnestly implore Him, saying, "Stay with us, for it is nearly evening and the day is almost over" (Lk 24:29). They welcome Him to table. Once at table, their roles get turned around. It is the paradox of the Incarnation. The guest becomes the host. As He did at the Last Supper, Jesus "took the bread, blessed and broke it, and gave it to them" (Lk 24:30). In that familiar gesture of self-giving love, they recognize the Lord and then He disappears. They no longer see His face, but Jesus stays with them, hidden in the breaking of the bread.

Notice. It is only when the two disciples take on the attitude of Jesus Himself, the attitude of generosity and welcome that their eyes are opened to His presence. Here is a profound truth about the Eucharist. The Risen Lord is truly present. When we come before Him, when we stay long enough, often enough, and still enough, He makes us generous and giving as He is. Before the Blessed Sacrament, we are not only right in His sight, but we become right in His sight.

Remaining in the Presence of Jesus in the Eucharist, gradually we become more like Him: more open, more caring and compassionate, and more welcoming to others. We become more giving, even to the point of sacrificing ourselves for others. Jesus waits for us in the Blessed Sacrament patiently until we come to have the same attitude He has for us. And then, when we do, Jesus reveals Himself to us. Our eyes are opened and our life becomes an Emmaus journey with the Lord.

> *The image of the disciples on the way to Emmaus can serve as a fitting guide... Amid our questions and difficulties, and even our bitter disappointments, the divine Wayfarer continues to walk at our side, opening to us the Scriptures and leading us to a deeper understanding of the mysteries of God. When we meet him fully, we will pass from the light of the Word to the light streaming from the "Bread of life", the supreme fulfilment of his promise to "be with us always, to the end of the age" (Mt 28:20).*
>
> Pope St. John Paul II,
> *Mane Nobiscum Domine*, 2

Prayer

Lord Jesus Christ,
stay with us, too, we pray,
in every part of our journey,
no matter how full of doubt
or fear we may be today.

Through your Holy Spirit,
we pray that you will open our eyes…
Help us see you as our risen Lord
in all your beauty
and in all your loving power. Amen.

May the heart of Jesus, in the Most Blessed Sacrament, be praised, adored, and loved with grateful affection, at every moment, in all the tabernacles of the world, even to the end of time. Amen.

Additional prayers begin on page 161

Conclusion

Across the oceans and the tides of time, at the heart of ancient Rome, there once stood a sports arena on the Vatican hill. In the year 37 A.D., the Emperor Caligula took an obelisk from Alexandria in Egypt and placed it on this spot. This stone rising 83 feet high and weighing 331 tons stood as a symbol of the power of Rome and the vast kingdom under Caesar. But, like every other kingdom, that great empire died with the death of the last Caesar.

Only once did a kingdom begin at the death of its king. At the death of Jesus, God's kingdom was ushered in the blood of the Lamb slain for our salvation. With the resurrection of the Crucified Jesus, God's kingdom began its march across the nations, lifting up the human family by the power of love. Now from every nation and race, there arises God's kingdom. It is vaster than any Caesar ever dreamed. It is a kingdom whose power will not die.

At the center of that kingdom is the source of its power. Not stone, not some empty symbol, but the Eucharist: the sacrifice and sacrament of love. As the Second Vatican Council teaches, "The Eucharist is the source and the summit of the Christian's life" (*Lumen Gentium*, 11).

Each time we gather to celebrate this great gift of the Eucharist, we repeat the words Jesus said at the Last Supper. Like the diamond in a ring surrounded by emeralds, these words are at the center of the Eucharistic Prayer the priest prays: "Take this, all of you, and eat of it, for this is my body which will be given up for you...Take this, all of you, and drink from it, for this is the chalice of my blood, the blood of the new and eternal covenant, which will be poured out for you and for many for the forgiveness of sins. Do this in memory of me" (Eucharistic Prayer III).

The priest says these words over the bread and wine. Bread and wine are significant. They are symbolic in the natural order. But, in the hands of Jesus, bread and wine are transformed not simply in meaning, but in fact. Bread broken, bread distributed, sharing in food, a sharing in life. Wine, the blood of the grape, flows as the grapes are crushed under foot like blood pouring from the defeated as they are trampled and trodden underfoot. Bread and wine, separate like the Body and the Blood separated in death on the Cross. By the power of Jesus' divine word, the bread and wine become truly His Body and His Blood.

Symbols fade. Reason fails. Only faith, the faith of the Church going back to the apostles in the Upper Room beneath the paschal moon, illumines the gift we are given. Simply stated, the Eucharist is the Lord Jesus. How profound the mystery! This is Jesus suffering and dying for us on the cross. This is Jesus whose body was broken and whose blood was outpoured for us sinners. Here eternity touches time and our poor humanity is flooded with the gift of divinity.

In all our lives there are many deserts we must face. In his Mass of Inauguration, Pope Benedict XVI listed a few. The desert of poverty. The desert of hunger and thirst. The desert of abandonment. Young or old, sinner or saint, we pass through many empty places where life is not valued, where love is not honored. There are moments in each of our lives where we sense loneliness, feel pain and hunger, and thirst for more. The Eucharist is our manna in the desert. As the Jews received the manna from heaven on their way to the Promised Land, we receive Jesus, the Bread of life.

He comes to strengthen us in our walk with God. He comes to dwell in us and share with us His life. We are never alone. Here is the meaning of communion in its deepest sense. As Jesus says at the Last Supper, "On that day you will know that I am in my Father and you in me, and I in you" (Jn 14:20). In every communion we are drawn up into the life of God. Holy Communion takes us up into the holiest communion: the sharing of the life of the Father, the Son, and the Holy Spirit.

And since God is love, every communion impels us to love. Receiving within ourselves this great sacrament of divine love and adoring it, we are moved to truly love one another. We are empowered to reach out to the lonely, the hungry, the hurting, to those close and those estranged. We are able to form bonds of love that make us a community. So while we can say, "No Eucharist, no Church," we can equally say, "Eucharist, Church."

In the Eucharist reserved in our churches, Jesus fulfills in a unique way the final words He ever spoke to His disciples in Matthew's gospel: "Behold, I am with you always, to the end of the world" (Mt 28:20). He stays with us as the Bread of life to nourish us during our earthly pilgrimage. And, as St. Ignatius of Antioch has said, Jesus offers Himself to us in the Eucharist as "the medicine of immortality" to preserve us from eternal death and prepare us for the resurrection of the body on the final day (*Letter to the Ephesians* 20:2).

His Real Presence in the Eucharist is His invitation to come to Him, to offer Him the adoration of our lives, to find strength and comfort to live as He teaches and to drink deeply of the wellsprings of salvation (Isa 12:3). As St. Thérèse of Lisieux once said, "Jesus is there in the tabernacle expressly for us... He burns with the desire to come into our hearts... He comes to find an empty tent within us—that is all He asks." Devout adoration of the Blessed Sacrament leads to a more perfect reception of Holy Communion. It deepens the mystery of our union with Christ. It so makes us one with Christ in loving all others that He can look to us and say, "This is my Body. This is my Blood."

Additional Prayers before the Blessed Sacrament

Act of Adoration

We adore You, Most Holy Lord, Jesus Christ, here and in all the churches of the whole world, and we bless You because by Your Cross You have redeemed the world. Have mercy on us.

St. Francis of Assisi

Act of Faith

I believe in my heart and openly profess that the bread and wine which are placed upon the altar are by the mystery of the sacred prayer and the words of the Redeemer substantially changed into the true and life-giving Flesh and Blood of Jesus Christ Our Lord and after the Consecration there is present the true Body of Christ which was born of the Virgin Mary and offered up for the salvation of the world, hung upon the Cross, and now sits at the right hand of the Father and there is present the true Blood of Christ which flowed from his side. They are present not only by means of a sign and of the efficacy of the Sacrament, but also in the very reality and truth of their nature and substance. Amen.

Saint Gregory VII

Prayer for Union with Christ

Lord Jesus Christ, pierce my soul with your love so that I may always long for you alone, who are the bread of angels and the fulfillment of the soul's deepest desires. May my heart always hunger and feed upon you so that my soul may be filled with the sweetness of your presence. May my soul thirst for you, who are the source of life, wisdom, knowledge, light and all the riches of God our Father. May I always seek and find you, think upon you, speak to you and do all things for the honor and glory of your holy name. Be always my only hope, my peace, my refuge and my help in whom my heart is rooted so that I may never be separated from you.

Saint Bonaventure

Prayer for Families

O Living Bread, that came down from heaven to give life to the world! O loving shepherd of our souls, from your throne of glory whence, a "hidden God", you pour out your grace upon families and peoples, we commend to you particularly the sick, the unhappy, the poor and all who beg for food and employment, imploring for all and every one the assistance of your providence; we commend to you the families, so that they may be fruitful centers of Christian life. May the abundance of your grace be poured over all. Amen.

Pope St. John XXIII

Prayer for Compassion

O Jesus, present in the Sacrament of the altar, teach all the nations to serve you with willing hearts, knowing that to serve God is to reign. May your sacrament, O Jesus, be light to the mind, strength to the will, joy to the heart. May it be the support of the weak, the comfort of the suffering, the wayfaring bread of salvation for the dying and for all the pledge of future glory. Amen.

Pope St. John XXIII

Act of Reparation

O Lord, my God and Savior,
as Thou didst endure for our salvation
the outrages of those who crucified Thee,
so now deign to bear with those
who by careless or unworthy Communions
approach and touch Thee,
not discerning Thee,
and endure all irreverences
rather than withhold Thy sacred Presence
from our Altars:
I bewail these indignities,
and most earnestly desire to prevent,
to the utmost of my power,

whatever thus still grieves Thee.
I beseech Thee,
accept this sorrow and this desire
as the only offering I can make
in reparation of so great dishonor.
O Lord, increase my faith,
and preserve me from the least profanation
of this adorable Mystery,
and kindle in me and in the hearts of all Thy people,
such reverence and devotion
that Thy most holy name may more and more be honored
and glorified in this Sacrament. Amen.

Scriptural Litany of the Holy Eucharist

Lord, have mercy — *Lord, have mercy*
Christ, have mercy — *Christ, have mercy*
Lord, have mercy — *Lord, have mercy*

Jesus, the Most High — *have mercy on us*
Jesus, the holy One — *have mercy on us*
Jesus, Word of God — *have mercy on us*
Jesus, only Son of the Father — *have mercy on us*
Jesus, Son of Mary — *have mercy on us*
Jesus, crucified for us — *have mercy on us*
Jesus, risen from the dead — *have mercy on us*
Jesus, reigning in glory — *have mercy on us*
Jesus, coming in glory — *have mercy on us*

Jesus, our Lord *have mercy on us*
Jesus, our hope *have mercy on us*
Jesus, our peace *have mercy on us*
Jesus, our Savior *have mercy on us*
Jesus, our salvation *have mercy on us*
Jesus, our resurrection *have mercy on us*

Jesus, Judge of all *have mercy on us*
Jesus, Lord of the Church *have mercy on us*
Jesus, Lord of creation *have mercy on us*
Jesus, Lover of all *have mercy on us*
Jesus, life of the world *have mercy on us*
Jesus, freedom for the imprisoned *have mercy on us*
Jesus, joy of the sorrowing *have mercy on us*
Jesus, giver of the Spirit *have mercy on us*
Jesus, giver of good gifts *have mercy on us*
Jesus, source of new life *have mercy on us*
Jesus, Lord of life *have mercy on us*
Jesus, eternal high priest *have mercy on us*
Jesus, priest and victim *have mercy on us*
Jesus, true Shepherd *have mercy on us*
Jesus, true Light *have mercy on us*
Jesus, bread of heaven *have mercy on us*
Jesus, bread of life *have mercy on us*
Jesus, bread of thanksgiving *have mercy on us*
Jesus, life-giving bread *have mercy on us*
Jesus, holy manna *have mercy on us*
Jesus, new covenant *have mercy on us*

Jesus, food for everlasting life *have mercy on us*
Jesus, food for our journey *have mercy on us*
Jesus, holy banquet *have mercy on us*
Jesus, true sacrifice *have mercy on us*
Jesus, perfect sacrifice *have mercy on us*
Jesus, eternal sacrifice *have mercy on us*
Jesus, divine Victim *have mercy on us*
Jesus, Mediator of the new covenant *have mercy on us*
Jesus, mystery of the altar *have mercy on us*
Jesus, medicine of immortality *have mercy on us*
Jesus, pledge of eternal glory *have mercy on us*

Jesus, Lamb of God,
you take away the sins of the world *have mercy on us*
Jesus, Bearer of our sins,
you take away the sins of the world *have mercy on us*
Jesus, Redeemer of the world,
you take away the sins of the world *have mercy on us*

Christ, hear us *Christ, hear us*
Christ, graciously hear us *Christ, graciously hear us*
Lord Jesus, hear our prayer *Lord Jesus, hear our prayer.*

Let us pray,
Lord our God,
in this great sacrament
we come into the presence of Jesus Christ, your Son,
born of the Virgin Mary and crucified for our salvation.
May we who declare our faith in this fountain of love
and mercy drink from it the water of everlasting life.

My Jesus, I believe that You are in the Blessed Sacrament. I love You above all things, and I long for You in my soul. Since I cannot now receive You sacramentally, come at least spiritually into my heart. As though You have already come, I embrace You and unite myself entirely to You; never permit me to be separated from You.

Litany of the Most Blessed Sacrament

St. Peter Julian Eymard

Lord, have mercy.
Lord, have mercy.
Christ, have mercy.
Christ, have mercy.
Lord, have mercy.
Lord, have mercy.

Christ, hear us.
Christ, graciously hear us.

God the Father of Heaven, *have mercy on us.*
God the Son, Redeemer of the world, *have mercy on us.*
God the Holy Spirit, *have mercy on us.*
Holy Trinity, one God, *have mercy on us.*

Jesus, Eternal High Priest of the Eucharistic Sacrifice, *have mercy on us.*
Jesus, Divine Victim on the Altar for our salvation, *have mercy on us.*
Jesus, hidden under the appearance of bread, *have mercy on us.*
Jesus, dwelling in the tabernacles of the world, *have mercy on us.*
Jesus, really, truly and substantially present in the Blessed Sacrament, *have mercy on us.*
Jesus, abiding in Your fullness, Body, Blood, Soul and Divinity, *have mercy on us.*
Jesus, Bread of Life, *have mercy on us.*
Jesus, Bread of Angels, *have mercy on us.*
Jesus, with us always until the end of the world, *have mercy on us.*

Sacred Host, summit and source of all worship and Christian life, *have mercy on us.*
Sacred Host, sign and cause of the unity of the Church, *have mercy on us.*
Sacred Host, adored by countless angels, *have mercy on us.*

Sacred Host, spiritual food, *have mercy on us.*

Sacred Host, Sacrament of love, *have mercy on us.*

Sacred Host, bond of charity, *have mercy on us.*

Sacred Host, greatest aid to holiness, *have mercy on us.*

Sacred Host, gift and glory of the priesthood, *have mercy on us.*

Sacred Host, in which we partake of Christ, *have mercy on us.*

Sacred Host, in which the soul is filled with grace, *have mercy on us.*

Sacred Host, in which we are given a pledge of future glory, *have mercy on us.*

Blessed be Jesus in the Most Holy Sacrament of the Altar.

Blessed be Jesus in the Most Holy Sacrament of the Altar.

Blessed be Jesus in the Most Holy Sacrament of the Altar.

For those who do not believe in Your Eucharistic presence, *have mercy, O Lord.*

For those who are indifferent to the Sacrament of Your love, *have mercy on us.*

For those who have offended You in the Holy Sacrament of the Altar, *have mercy on us.*

That we may show fitting reverence when entering Your holy temple, *we beseech You, hear us.*

That we may make suitable preparation before approaching the Altar, *we beseech You, hear us.*

That we may receive You frequently in Holy Communion with real devotion and true humility, *we beseech You, hear us.*

That we may never neglect to thank You for so wonderful a blessing, *we beseech You, hear us.*

That we may cherish time spent in silent prayer before You, *we beseech You, hear us.*

That we may grow in knowledge of this Sacrament of sacraments, *we beseech You, hear us.*

That all priests may have a profound love of the Holy Eucharist, *we beseech You, hear us.*

That they may celebrate the Holy Sacrifice of the Mass in accordance with its sublime dignity, *we beseech You, hear us.*

That we may be comforted and sanctified with Holy Viaticum at the hour of our death, *we beseech You, hear us.*

That we may see You one day face to face in Heaven, *we beseech You, hear us.*

Lamb of God, You take away the sins of the world, *spare us, O Lord.*

Lamb of God, You take away the sins of the world, *graciously hear us, O Lord.*

Lamb of God, You take away the sins of the world, *have mercy on us, O Lord.*

℣. O Sacrament Most Holy, O Sacrament Divine,

℟. all praise and all thanksgiving be every moment Thine.

Let us pray,

Most merciful Father,
You continue to draw us to Yourself
through the Eucharistic Mystery.
Grant us fervent faith in this Sacrament of love,
in which Christ the Lord Himself is contained, offered and received.
Through the same Christ our Lord. ℟. Amen.

Divine Praises

Blessed be God.
Blessed be His Holy Name.
Blessed be Jesus Christ, true God and true Man.
Blessed be the Name of Jesus.
Blessed be His Most Sacred Heart.
Blessed be His Most Precious Blood.
Blessed be Jesus in the Most Holy Sacrament of the Altar.

Blessed be the Holy Spirit, the Paraclete.
Blessed be the great Mother of God, Mary most Holy.
Blessed be her Holy and Immaculate Conception.
Blessed be her Glorious Assumption.
Blessed be the name of Mary, Virgin and Mother.
Blessed be St. Joseph, her most chaste spouse.
Blessed be God in His Angels and in His Saints. Amen.

Scripture Passages on the Eucharist

THE MIRACLE OF THE MULTIPLICATION OF LOAVES AND FISH for the 5,000 (Mt 14:13-21; Mk 6:31-44; Lk 9:12-17; Jn 6:1-14).

THE MIRACLE OF THE MULTIPLICATION OF LOAVES AND FISH for the 4,000 (Mt 15:32-39; Mk 8:1-9)

JESUS' TEACHING ON THE EUCHARIST IN THE SYNAGOGUE OF CAPERNAUM (Jn 6:22-71)

THE INSTITUTION OF THE EUCHARIST AT THE LAST SUPPER (Mt 26:26-30; Mk 14:17-26; Lk 22: 14-20)

THE APPEARANCE OF THE RISEN JESUS ON THE ROAD TO EMMAUS (Lk 24:13-35)

PAUL'S TEACHING OF THE EUCHARIST (1 Cor 11:17-29)

THE EUCHARIST IN THE POST-PASCHAL COMMUNITY (ACTS 2:40-42)

THE SUPPER OF THE LAMB (Rev 19:6-9)

Bishop Emeritus Arthur J. Serratelli was the seventh bishop of the Diocese of Paterson, N.J. He is present chairman for the Vatican's Dialogue between the Catholic Church and the World Alliance of Baptists. He has served as chairman of the International Commission on English in the Liturgy; member of the Vatican's Congregation of Divine Worship and the Discipline of the Sacraments; and member of Vox Clara. He has served a three-year term as chairman of the Committee for the Translation of Sacred Scripture of the United States Conference of Catholic Bishops; twice chairman of the Committee on Divine Worship of the United States Conference of Catholic Bishops; chairman of the Committee on Doctrine; and member of the Subcommittee for the Review of Catechetical Texts. As a Professor of Sacred Scripture and Systematics, he has taught in three major seminaries. He continues to give retreats, lectures, and courses in Sacred Scripture as well as doing pastoral work in a parish.

This is the Bishop's sixth book. His previous books are: *From the Cross to the Empty Tomb*, *The Seven Gifts of the Holy Spirit*, *Jesus' Last Days*, *The Parables of Jesus* and *Scriptural Novena to St. Joseph*.

Books by Most Rev. Arthur J. Serratelli, S.T.D., S.S.L., D.D.

JESUS' LAST DAYS

Through Bishop Serratelli's reflections on the similar accounts of the four evangelists, we relive Jesus' Passion bathed in the light of Easter glory. We will appreciate how the Cross remains the instrument of our salvation and see more clearly our own call to discipleship. 128 pages. Size 5 x 7.

No. 932/04—Flexible cover.................. **9.95**

ISBN 978-1-9-47070-35-6

POCKET CATECHISM ON THE EUCHARIST WITH PRAYERS

RCIA candidates, non-practicing Catholics, and daily communicants all have something to learn from the brief but orthodox responses to the 21 most-asked questions about the Eucharist. This little catechism is a most useful resource in the accurate transmission of the Catholic Faith. Be an evangelizer by passing on copies.

48 pages. Size 4 x 6 $^{1}/_{2}$.

No. 71/04—Self-cover.. **3.95**

ISBN 978-1-953152-87-9

THE SEVEN GIFTS OF THE HOLY SPIRIT

Through history, art, Scripture, and Catholic documents, you will appreciate and grasp more fully how the seven gifts of the Holy Spirit can help you to live a truly authentic Christian life filled with peace and joy. 96 pages. Size 4 $^{3}/_{8}$ x 6 $^{3}/_{4}$.

No. 930/04—Flexible cover **8.00**

ISBN 978-1-947070-23-3

FROM THE CROSS TO THE EMPTY TOMB

Most Rev. Arthur J. Serratelli, S.T.D., S.S.L., D.D.

The author invites you to journey with those who were with Jesus in His last hours. You may be like Peter one day, and like Judas, Simon, Mary Magdalene, or Our Lady on another. This Lenten book provides a deeper appreciation for God's eternal saving love.
96 pages. Size 4 3/8 x 6 3/4.

No. 928/04—Flexible cover **7.95**
ISBN 978-1-947070-13-4

THE PARABLES OF JESUS

Most Rev. Arthur J. Serratelli, S.T.D., S.S.L., D.D.

Follow Jesus through His interaction with farmers, shepherds, aristocrats, religious and political leaders, and laborers in 13 parables filled with contrast, exaggeration, humor, and surprise that represent more than one third of His teachings. Both the scholar and student, the expert and the layperson can draw inspiration from the greatest storyteller the world has ever known. Even lifetime Catholics who think they know the parables will be rewarded with the wisdom and history that the author shares on these beloved, grace-filled stories.
176 pages. Size 5 1/4 x 7 3/4.

No. 934/04—Flexible cover.. **8.95**
ISBN 978-1-953152-08-4

SCRIPTURAL NOVENA TO JESUS IN THE BLESSED SACRAMENT

Most Rev. Arthur J. Serratelli, S.T.D., S.S.L., D.D.

Holy Scripture, a Novena to Jesus, and the Blessed Sacrament—mainstays of our Catholic Faith—are perfectly united in this elegant prayer book. It will help you understand, celebrate, and live the Eucharist and to adore Jesus truly present in the Blessed Sacrament.
128 pages. Size 4 3/8 x 6 3/4.

No. 948/19—Dura-Lux cover....... **11.95**
ISBN 978-1-953152-82-4

SCRIPTURAL NOVENA TO SAINT JOSEPH

Most Rev. Arthur J. Serratelli, S.T.D., S.S.L., D.D.

Written with deep devotion and respect for Jesus' earthly father, these nine biblical reflections will help you to grow in your knowledge and love of the Church's holy patron, St. Joseph.

You, your family, and the Church will be blessed by praying to the holy, humble, just, and trustworthy St. Joseph. He has the power to assist and protect us as he did most perfectly for Mary and their Son.
96 pages. Size 4 3/8 x 6 3/4.

No. 946/04—Paperback cover....................................... **7.00**
ISBN 978-1-953152-30-5